D0278692

Reese Witherspoon

Reese Witherspoon

PEOPLE
IN THE NEWS

Reese
Witherspoon

by Anne E. Hill

**LUCENT
BOOKS**®

THOMSON

™

GALE

San Diego • Detroit • New York • San Francisco • Cleveland
New Haven, Conn. • Waterville, Maine • London • Munich

THOMSON

✳

™

GALE

LIBRARY OF CONGRESS CATALOGING-IN-PUBLICATION DATA

Hill, Anne E., 1974–
    Reese Witherspoon / by Anne E. Hill.
        p. cm. — (People in the news)
Summary: A biography of Reese Witherspoon, the award-winning motion picture actress known for her work in *Legally Blonde*, *Sweet Home Alabama*, and *Election*.
Includes bibliographical references and index.
        ISBN 1-59018-450-5 (hardback : alk. paper)
        1. Witherspoon, Reese, 1976—Juvenile literature. 2. Motion picture actors and ac-
tresses—United States—Biography—Juvenile literature. [1. Witherspoon, Reese, 1976—
2. Actors and actresses. 3. Women—Biography.] I. Title. II. Series.
        PN2287.W54H55 2004
        791.43′028′092—dc21
                                                                                                2003007296

Printed in the United States of America

For George and Caleb,
the men in my life

Table of Contents

Foreword

FAME AND CELEBRITY are alluring. People are drawn to those who walk in fame's spotlight, whether they are known for great accomplishments or for notorious deeds. The lives of the famous pique public interest and attract attention, perhaps because their experiences seem in some ways so different from, yet in other ways so similar to, our own.

Newspapers, magazines, and television regularly capitalize on this fascination with celebrity by running profiles of famous people. For example, television programs such as *Entertainment Tonight* devote all of their programming to stories about entertainment and entertainers. Magazines such as *People* fill their pages with stories of the private lives of famous people. Even newspapers, newsmagazines, and television news frequently delve into the lives of well-known personalities. Despite the number of articles and programs, few provide more than a superficial glimpse at their subjects.

Lucent's People in the News series offers young readers a deeper look into the lives of today's newsmakers, the influences that have shaped them, and the impact they have had in their fields of endeavor and on other people's lives. The subjects of the series hail from many disciplines and walks of life. They include authors, musicians, athletes, political leaders, entertainers, entrepreneurs, and others who have made a mark on modern life and who, in many cases, will continue to do so for years to come.

These biographies are more than factual chronicles. Each book emphasizes the contributions, accomplishments, or deeds that have brought fame or notoriety to the individual and shows how that person has influenced modern life. Authors portray their subjects in a realistic, unsentimental light. For example, Bill Gates— the cofounder and chief executive officer of the software giant Microsoft—has been instrumental in making personal computers the most vital tool of the modern age. Few dispute his business savvy, his perseverance, or his technical expertise, yet critics say he is ruthless in his dealings with competitors and driven more by his desire to maintain Microsoft's dominance in the computer industry than by an interest in furthering technology.

In these books, young readers will encounter inspiring stories about real people who achieved success despite enormous obstacles. Oprah Winfrey—the most powerful, most watched, and wealthiest woman on television today—spent the first six years of her life in the care of her grandparents while her unwed mother sought work and a better life elsewhere. Her adolescence was colored by promiscuity, pregnancy at age fourteen, rape, and sexual abuse.

Each author documents and supports his or her work with an array of primary and secondary source quotations taken from diaries, letters, speeches, and interviews. All quotes are footnoted to show readers exactly how and where biographers derive their information and provide guidance for further research. The quotations enliven the text by giving readers eyewitness views of the life and accomplishments of each person covered in the People in the News series.

In addition, each book in the series includes photographs, annotated bibliographies, timelines, and comprehensive indexes. For both the casual reader and the student researcher, the People in the News series offers insight into the lives of today's newsmakers—people who shape the way we live, work, and play in the modern age.

Introduction

America's Newest Sweetheart

IT WAS THE surprise hit of the summer of 2001. The frothy comedy *Legally Blonde* grossed nearly $100 million at the box office and made a star of Reese Witherspoon. Her portrayal as sorority-girl-turned-lawyer Elle Woods seemed to take everyone by surprise. Suddenly, people wanted to know about Witherspoon. She was being called the next Julia Roberts, the Academy Award–winning actress who is known for her ability to make movies that gross more than $100 million.

But what Americans did not know was that their newest sweetheart was not a newcomer to Hollywood at all. She had been acting for more than a decade. She got her first job at age fourteen when she auditioned to be an extra in the film *The Man in the Moon* and ended up winning the lead role. Other roles followed and she built an impressive résumé while keeping a low profile in Hollywood. Her career had been filled with critical success as well as some flops. But she had not had a big role in a high-profile movie to make her well known to moviegoers. "I've been like a snail crawling my way to this point," Witherspoon told a reporter in 2002. "And I think all the failure that I had in the past 13 years really helped me appreciate the moment that I'm in."[1]

Witherspoon's determination to find the right roles has paid off as she has been able to play a variety of characters and be convincing in each part. She has played everything from a high school girl who will do anything to be senior class president in *Election* to a compassionate stripper in *Overnight Delivery* to an innocent virgin vowing to wait for marriage in *Cruel Intentions*.

And while critics may have taken notice of the petite blond, audiences were slower to come around. That suited Witherspoon just fine. She has placed family over her career since marrying actor Ryan Phillippe and having daughter Ava in 1999. Since starting a family, Witherspoon has taken time off and now makes only one film a year. She has also managed never to be away from her husband for more than two weeks at a time. Together, Witherspoon and Phillippe have managed to create a successful Hollywood marriage while raising their daughter and working in a highly competitive field.

Reese Witherspoon and her husband Ryan Phillippe arrive at a movie premiere in 2002. Reese places her family above her acting career.

But Witherspoon is the first to say her life is not perfect. "I'm not interested in the fallacy of the Hollywood relationship: 'We have perfect children who never cry; we never have problems; we never argue, we're always best friends,'" she says. "That's just not true. We're normal people with normal problems."[2]

Witherspoon's normalcy may be part of the reason she is so popular with audiences. She seems like someone who would be easy to get to know and fun to be around. But while Reese Witherspoon may seem like an average person, she is now taking home a paycheck for millions per movie that puts her in a league with the likes of Julia Roberts, Jennifer Lopez, and Cameron Diaz. She is now a certified movie star.

But unlike many big-name actors, Reese Witherspoon has vowed to keep playing unique characters in interesting films and not take just any script that comes her way promising a big paycheck. Anxious to find good scripts featuring women, as well as to create positive roles for other female actresses, Witherspoon has even started her own film company. She hopes to make quality movies—movies that she would want her own daughter to see someday. She wants to make a difference in Hollywood, but not at the sacrifice of the things she really holds dear—her family and ideals of honest, hard work and being true to herself. "If it were gone tomorrow, would it change who I am? No," Witherspoon says. "I'll be a little disappointed. It will be hard to pick myself up, but I could do it."[3]

Not that failure seems part of Reese Witherspoon's future. She has successfully combined marriage, children, and career. And she is giving the other actresses in Hollywood a lot to live up to.

Chapter 1

Sweet Home Tennessee

Nashville, Tennessee, is a long way from Hollywood. It seemed unlikely that a girl like Reese Witherspoon would ever be a successful actress. But Witherspoon was born into a family that believed in her and told her she could do anything she wanted, so she got started early and was able to pursue acting. She starred in local television commercials as a child before getting her break in films as a teen.

Reese was born Laura Jean Reese Witherspoon in New Orleans, Louisiana, on March 22, 1976, to John and Betty Witherspoon. She was called Reese, however, her mother's maiden name. Reese was the baby of the family. Her brother John Jr. is three years older.

The Witherspoon family was constantly on the move in Reese's early years. The elder John Witherspoon, a surgeon, was a lieutenant colonel in the army reserves, and the family moved from town to town depending upon where he was stationed. They spent much of Reese's early childhood in Germany and other parts of Europe before finally settling down in Nashville, Tennessee, when Reese was five years old.

Southern Living

The Witherspoons were an upper-middle-class family with a distinguished past. Their Scottish ancestor, John Witherspoon, even signed the Declaration of Independence and was the first president of Princeton University. The Reese family was southern gentility, privileged people from Tennessee and Virginia. The two families became intertwined when John and Betty met while attending the University of Tennessee in Knoxville, married, and started a family of their own.

John Witherspoon

Reese Witherspoon's ancestor, Reverend John Witherspoon, was born in Gifford, Scotland, in 1722. He received a fine education, attending a preparatory school and earning a master of arts degree at Edinburgh and a doctorate of divinity from the University of Saint Andrews.

In 1768 Witherspoon became the first president of the College of New Jersey (now known as Princeton University) and served until 1792. He was incredibly popular as president and turned the college into a successful institute of higher learning.

He also wrote many essays on colonial life and came to adopt the revolutionary cause. In 1776 he was elected as a delegate to the Continental Congress, where he voted in favor of independence from England. He signed the Declaration of Independence and became an active member of Congress. He served on over one hundred committees and loved a lively debate. He was also twice elected to the state legislature of New Jersey.

In late 1776 he was forced to evacuate the college as British forces approached and nearly destroyed it. Witherspoon dedicated the rest of his life to rebuilding the school and serving his country in government.

He died on Tusculum, his farm just outside of Princeton, New Jersey, in November 1794. Visitors to Princeton can walk down Witherspoon Street, a main street in the town, that was named after John Witherspoon.

Reverend John Witherspoon, Reese's ancestor, was a writer, politician, and champion of education in the early United States.

While Reese is proud of her family's history, she seems to take more interest in her family of today. She grew up very close to her father, mother (who has a Ph.D. in pediatric nursing), and brother. She has proudly called her family eccentric. "There was always a sense of humor in our family," she recalls. "My mom was a very positive woman who was also very funny and silly, a Southern eccentric."[4]

Her father also had a fun side. He was not just a serious doctor. "My father . . . rides a Harley [motorcycle] and wears camouflage gear everywhere," she told a reporter in 2002.[5]

For the Witherspoons, family came first. Betty and John urged their children to develop their own interests. Reese grew up knowing that they would support her in whatever she decided to do—whether it was Girl Scouts, cheerleading, gymnastics, or acting.

The Witherspoons also stressed being polite and kind and to always say "please" and "thank you." Reese even took manners and etiquette classes when she was a little girl. Because of her family, Reese learned some of her life's most important lessons early on. She claims, "My Southern upbringing has been real beneficial to me in this industry; being conscientious about people's feelings, being polite, being responsible and never taking for granted what you have in your life."[6]

Little Type A

Reese was very serious and responsible from the start. Her mother even dubbed her "Little Type A" because Reese was so serious as a child. (People with type A personalities are considered organized, competitive, and aggressive.)

She was also ambitious. When Reese was just three years old, she taught herself how to read. When Reese enrolled at school, two years later, she was far ahead of the other kids. She recalls, "I got to kindergarten and they called my mother and said, 'Do you know your daughter can read every single book we have here?' They were shocked."[7] Reese claims that she always loved to study and read and still does, even as an adult.

Even though Reese likes to study and excel at her activities, she was still a typical kid who liked to play outside and get dirty. She was a tomboy who wore her brother's old clothes and scraped up her knees.

"I Wanted to Be an Actor"

Reese was also a ham. She loved to be a clown and get the attention of her classmates. That talent translated into a desire to

perform for larger audiences. She confessed that her first ambition was to be a country-and-western singer like Dolly Parton.
Even today, she has great admiration for the singer. But Reese
changed her mind and decided to become an actress when she
was just seven years old. "There was a little girl who lived down
the street and her parents owned a flower shop, and they asked
me to be in their local commercial and I was just . . . bit [by
the acting bug]," she recalls. "I came home and told my mother
I wanted to be an actress. It all came from me. It was all self-
generated."[8]

Although Reese was young, her parents took her seriously
and helped her get started. Reese remembers:

> My parents were both physicians and they thought that
> was a very strange choice for a little girl from Tennessee,
> but they were always really cool about it. If it was some-
> thing I wanted to do they would drive me to lessons. I just
> always really appreciated that because you don't ever feel
> restricted or like your dreams are stupid. . . . My family
> are the most proud people that they supported me and
> they just always reveled in my success because they al-
> ways were just very open minded about things.[9]

Reese went on auditions and appeared in several local television commercials for area businesses. But Nashville did not have
a lot of professional acting opportunities for kids, so Reese was
mostly limited to putting on shows with friends, appearing in
school plays, and taking acting lessons at the local community college, which her parents faithfully drove her to each week.

The Man in the Moon

Reese never imagined that Hollywood would come to Nashville
and that she would get her big break. Movies were rarely filmed
in the southern city and celebrity sightings (except for country
music stars) were rare. But when Reese was fourteen, she spot-
ted an ad in the local paper calling for extras in a movie called
The Man in the Moon that was shooting that summer in the Nashville
area. Intrigued, Reese decided to audition. What she did not ex-
pect was to be called back to read for the lead role of Dani, a young

teen and tomboy growing up in the South in the 1950s who is experiencing her first love.

The film's director, Robert Mulligan, had an eye for finding young talent. He had directed three young children in the critically acclaimed 1960 movie *To Kill a Mockingbird*, based on the book by Harper Lee. And he saw something special in Reese. After having her read for the part again, Mulligan decided to cast Reese as the lead. The Witherspoons were shocked when they got the telephone call with the news. Reese's dream was coming true and she was thrilled.

So instead of spending a week or two filling the back of the screen as an extra, Reese spent the summer of 1990 in both Tennessee and Louisiana as the star of a major motion picture. She showed incredible talent and concentration from the start and her costars, who included Sam Waterston and Jason London, were impressed that the teen was professional despite not having much experience. Costar Tess Harper, who played Reese's mom in the film, told *US Weekly* magazine, "[Reese] had the quiet sophistication of an adult. We nicknamed her Little Meryl after Meryl Streep. She was, and is, that good. I can definitely see her winning an Oscar."[10]

Reese Witherspoon shares a tender on-screen moment with costar Jason London in her first leading role in The Man in the Moon.

Reese was also very mature about how to spend the money she made from the movie. At her parents' urging, all but one hundred dollars was deposited into a savings account earmarked for her college education. Reese and her best friend took the remaining money and went to The Gap, where they went on a shopping spree. Reese claims she cannot remember what she bought but says it was probably black because her parents would not buy her black clothes.

Despite her positive experience making *The Man in the Moon* and the natural talent she displayed, Reese did not have any plans to continue making movies. "It was a wonderful opportunity to work with a brilliant director," she said. "I went to Louisiana and made the movie and thought, 'Well, that was fun.' But I didn't know if I'd ever do it again."[11]

A Nervous Audition

But other people had big plans for Reese. The cinematographer for *The Man in the Moon* was going to work next with director Martin Scorsese on the film *Cape Fear*. There was a part for a teenage girl in the movie that had not yet been cast and he recommended that Scorsese audition Reese Witherspoon.

Even though Reese was not convinced that she would ever have a career as an actress, she was having fun. So she decided to

Reese on Peer Pressure

Like most teens, Reese Witherspoon had run-ins with peer pressure. In the article "Reese's Pieces," she tells Elizabeth Kuster of *CosmoGirl!* magazine:

There was a time early on in high school when there was a lot of pressure to be mean. You were part of the cool crowd if you were mean-spirited toward other people. I remember my mom— one day she came home, and my best friend and I were being so mean about somebody, saying we thought they were a dork or something. I remember my mom saying, "That's the most awful thing! I don't want you speaking like that in my house." And I thought Oh, Mom. Whatever. It was the cool thing to do—tear other people down. I think that's so uncool now. You do it because you're so completely insecure about yourself that you can't be cool about other people.

travel to New York to audition for Scorsese and the film's lead, Academy Award–winning actor Robert De Niro. The meeting did not go well though. She recalls:

> I had never heard of Robert De Niro or Martin Scorsese. But I was only 14. . . . But my mother got me all dressed up and put me on the airplane for my big trip to New York City. I wasn't nervous, because I didn't know who these people were. Then I sat next to a man on the plane and told him I was going to New York to read for a movie. I was so proud. When I told him who I was reading for, he almost had a heart attack. He was going crazy. He told me they were the most important acting-directing team of our time. I started shaking and didn't stop shaking until the audition was over. I was shaking so bad at the audition that De Niro had to finish my lines. Needless to say, I didn't get the part (Juliette Lewis got it), and I doubt whether Mr. Martin Scorsese remembers little Miss Reese Witherspoon.[12]

Teenage Actress

Reese did not let the experience deter her, however. Over the next two years, she went to many more auditions and appeared in three television movies. The first was called *Wildflower* and was directed by actress Diane Keaton. It told the story of a partially deaf and abused girl who is helped by two young children. The second was *Desperate Choices: To Save My Child,* which starred Joanna Kerns, the mother from the hit 1980s series *Growing Pains.* In the film, Reese plays a young girl who is diagnosed with bone marrow cancer.

The third, a made-for-television miniseries entitled *Return to Lonesome Dove,* aired in 1993 and taught Reese that there were some big differences between movies and television. Reese remembers: "It was nice; we sort of dressed up and rode around on horses for a while. It's really rigorous shooting television, though, and I've stopped doing it because it's a really hard schedule to keep up with. It's a lot tougher than being on a movie; you don't have a lot of time to get into your character or prepare, or feel like you're doing a good job."[18]

Witherspoon and Oliver Reed pose for a publicity shot for the made-for-television miniseries Return to Lonesome Dove. *The frantic pace of shooting television prompted Reese to focus on making movies.*

Reese enjoyed her work in two films for the big screen and decided that was the kind of acting she wanted to pursue. In 1993 she starred in *Jack the Bear* with Danny DeVito (in which she plays a twelve-year-old girl) and *A Far Off Place*, a Disney movie about a young girl and boy who survive the killing of a family of gamekeepers and are forced to travel across the African desert with the murderers at their heels.

Although Reese had good luck at auditions, she was turned down for parts as well. She took it all in stride, even at an age when rejection can feel especially bitter and disappointing. "I handle rejection pretty well," she says. "I never take it personally. If I don't get a job, I believe I wasn't meant to get that job. You get the jobs you were meant to get."[14]

All the money for the jobs Reese did get was deposited into a savings account for college. Reese's parents were proud that their daughter was being so responsible and would be able to pay her way at the school of her choice.

The Debutante

In the middle of high school, Reese took time off from acting—but just to fulfill a family obligation. The Witherspoons were natives of the South, and it was a longstanding tradition that the women in the family debut or "come out." Most of Reese's classmates were also being presented at parties which historically meant they were now able to marry.

Reese herself did not yet feel ready for marriage and she did not have a steady boyfriend. Still, she went through with the ritual. She says, "I did the whole thing—big white dress, white gloves, and all. You don't really think about it when you're in the midst of it, but now that I'm older, I look back and think, 'Well, that was kind of crazy.' But it's really about tradition. My family had done it for a long time, so I was following in a long line of Witherspoons." [15]

High School

While Reese may have fit in and looked like all the other debutantes, she was different from the other girls. She had met famous actors and worked with well-known directors. During her breaks, instead of shopping and sleeping late, she traveled all over the country making movies. It was as if Reese were living a double

Reese's Prom Date

Reese Witherspoon attended an all-girls school, but not having boys in classes made getting dates for dances and proms difficult. In the article "Reese's Pieces," she tells reporter Elizabeth Kuster of *CosmoGirl!* magazine:

> Senior prom was a weird situation. I went to an all-girl high school, so I had to do the asking. I asked this boy who was a junior. Everyone was supposed to meet at my house—and he didn't show up. It was getting later and later and later, and finally my dad put on his tux and was ready to take me. Then the guy shows up like "Oh sorry." Like it was no big deal. It was my senior prom! I ended up going with him but he officially lost his name. For the rest of my senior year, we just called him "Prom Date." My friends even made these pins that had his face on them, with the words I LOVE PROM DATE!

life. She lived like an average teenager at home in Nashville, but that life was occasionally interrupted by trips to Los Angeles or New York for auditions.

Most of Reese's good friends at Nashville's private and exclusive all-girls school, Harpeth Hall, were proud of their friend but others were jealous of her success. Reese, however, did her best to fit in and participate in academics and extracurricular activities. "She was brilliant, always straight A-plus in everything she did," classmate Heather Hodde told *US Weekly* magazine.[16]

A smiling Reese poses at her high school formal in 1994. As a young actress, Witherspoon sometimes found it difficult to be a typical teenager.

Reese's art teacher, Carol Chambers, claims, "She was a social young lady always in the thick of things. She liked to talk—maybe a little too much."[17]

But Reese claims she was just as socially awkward as she was social. She sucked her thumb until she was eleven and wore glasses. She worried about her hair and clothes. Reese is thankful she had to wear a uniform to school every day so she need not agonize over or be judged on her wardrobe.

But while she had normal teenage worries and concerns, Reese also stood up for others and spoke her mind. Schoolmate Allison Hodde remembers how kind she was. "I was one of the underdogs," she explains. "Kids picked on me because I had a learning disability. If I was sad, [Reese] would always notice. She'd put her arm around me and say, 'Don't worry about them.'"[18]

In addition to making friends and defending them, Reese spent a lot of time studying. She was a self-professed bookworm. And all of her studying paid off in her senior year when she was accepted to the prestigious Stanford University in Palo Alto, California. Thanks to all of her hard work acting, she also had enough money to pay her own way.

Reese spent the summer after graduation making another movie, *S.F.W.*, about teens held hostage in a local convenience store for thirty-six days. They then become celebrities when they are finally released.

Once she finished filming, Reese started getting ready to move to California. The student in her was excited to be headed to such a good school, while the actress in her was happy that she would be closer to Los Angeles in case any good roles came her way during breaks.

Chapter 2

Actress and Student

WHEN WITHERSPOON LEFT for college, she had planned to juggle the demands of being both a full-time student and a part-time actress. But making movies claimed more of her time almost from the start. Although she was not convinced acting would be her career, it was her passion—and she made quite a bit of money doing it. This was a good thing because Witherspoon claims she would not have continued acting if she had had to struggle. Witherspoon says, "I probably wouldn't have pursued acting if it hadn't fallen into my lap like it did. If I had to move to L.A. and live in my car, I would not have acted. It's not practical enough."[19]

Practical Witherspoon was determined to go to college and her parents were adamant that she finish her education. So Witherspoon was ready to be both an actress and student—almost.

Freeway

Witherspoon delayed heading to Stanford for a year (until September 1995) so she could take on two more acting jobs. The first was a starring role with Kiefer Sutherland in the independent film *Freeway*, which is loosely based on the classic children's story "Little Red Riding Hood." In *Freeway*, Witherspoon plays a tough high school girl named Vanessa Lutz who is on her way to her grandmother's house. Vanessa gets picked up by Bob Wolverton, a man who seems like he can help her out. But he is a killer bent on seeing Vanessa dead. After she escapes, Vanessa has to prove she was his victim and that she was justified in killing him.

The role of Vanessa Lutz was the most satisfying acting experience Witherspoon had had so far because she pushed herself farther than she had ever done before. "That's when I finally totally got what acting was about—dissolving into my work rather than being conscious of myself and how I looked," she says.[20]

The role earned her high praise. Witherspoon's director on the film, Matthew Bright, said, "I don't think there's anything she couldn't do [in terms of acting]."[21] And critic James Berardinelli of ReelViews said Witherspoon "displays an aptitude for acting naturally and believably, no matter how outrageous her circumstances are. She captivates with her nonstop energy, culling our sympathy and enabling us to see the world through Vanessa's eyes."[22]

International audiences were impressed as well. Witherspoon won the Best Actress Award at the Spanish Catalonian International Film Festival, which also nominated *Freeway* for the Best Film Award. In fact, the performance is still considered one of Witherspoon's best to date.

Fear

In Witherspoon's next film, she played someone very different from Vanessa Lutz. As an innocent high school student in the

Witherspoon appears in a scene from Freeway, *a movie that offered the star one of her most challenging acting roles.*

Witherspoon and Mark Wahlberg in a scene from the thriller Fear. *Reese took the role because thrillers are her favorite movie genre.*

film *Fear*, Witherspoon's character, Nicole Walker, gets involved with a young man she does not realize is both obsessive and dangerous.

Witherspoon chose to make the movie because she had never done a thriller, which is her favorite movie genre. She also felt the movie had an important message. Witherspoon explains, "I saw a lot of my girlfriends get into obsessive relationships as teenagers. The film shows people can make mistakes and they can be fatal."[23]

Actor Mark Wahlberg plays the part of David, Nicole's violent boyfriend. In the film, David ends up dead, like so many other objects of Witherspoon's characters' affection (her boyfriends in *The Man in the Moon* and other films also ended up being killed). "People should know better than to play my boyfriend in the movies," Witherspoon joked with a reporter in 1996.[24] Witherspoon and Wahlberg were also rumored to have dated during filming, but Witherspoon never confirmed or denied the rumors.

After finishing work on *Fear*, Witherspoon left for college. It was even harder for her to leave for school after the positive acting experience she had had, especially on *Freeway*. But she kept her promise to her parents and herself and made the trip halfway across the country to Palo Alto, California.

College Days

Witherspoon arrived at Stanford in September 1995. When she got there, Witherspoon put her scripts away at least temporarily and threw herself into college life. She was just as nervous as every other college freshman at first. She admitted she cried her first day at school and was scared that no one would eat dinner with her. Luckily, she adjusted and made some new friends. Her hall mate Liz McDade-Montez even became her personal assistant while she was at school.

Witherspoon was soon happy to be part of the thriving academic community at Stanford. But she was not sure what she should study. While acting would have seemed a logical choice, Witherspoon wanted to branch out. She was considering either

Celebrities at Stanford

Stanford University, one of the top-ranked colleges in the country, is known as an academically rigorous school. It has also had many famous students. News anchor Ted Koppel, writer John Steinbeck, first daughter Chelsea Clinton, and golfer Tiger Woods are just a few of the famous people who have attended Stanford. In fact, when Reese Witherspoon was a student, Tiger Woods, Olympic gymnast Dominique Dawes, and actor Fred Savage were also enrolled.

With so many famous faces wandering around campus, Witherspoon was surprised that she was ever recognized. In 1997 Witherspoon talked with Michele Keller of *Seventeen* magazine about Stanford students knowing who she was. She said, "I think the movies I did up until then were pretty much targeted for that age group. I had never been in a place where the group was so concentrated. Everybody [on campus] knew me by different characters, which surprised me."

premed, so she could be a doctor like her parents, or anthropology. She told *InStyle* magazine in 2002 that she enjoys anthropology because she likes figuring out what makes people tick. She said, "How people live, what they eat, what's aesthetically pleasing to them—I'm so interested in all that stuff."[25] Finally, Witherspoon decided to major in English literature because she loved reading and writing.

Witherspoon enjoyed her academic life at Stanford because she was able to study and write papers all day. "I was a pretty good student," Witherspoon claims. "I was always busy on some sort of tangent thinking about other things, not what was at hand. I was a last minute kind of person but I loved writing papers, researching, being in the library. I loved that kind of stuff."[26]

Juggling Act

Witherspoon had to admit she was torn between studying and acting. She wanted to continue with college, but acting opportunities were plentiful. Witherspoon was being asked to audition for many films and was being offered good roles.

Because she was so busy at school, Witherspoon was selective about the projects she took on. She had little time to participate in any of the extracurricular activities offered at Stanford. Instead, she read many scripts in her free time. When she decided on one that required her to take a few weeks off from school, Witherspoon made a choice.

She traveled to Minnesota in the middle of her winter quarter to make the film *Overnight Delivery*. Liz McDade-Montez came along with Witherspoon as both a friend and assistant and appeared onscreen as an extra in the film.

In the romantic comedy *Overnight Delivery*, Witherspoon plays a stripper, somewhat reluctantly. She does not like to play strippers or prostitutes because these are not the kinds of characters she wants young girls seeing her movies to be influenced by. She wants to present women in a different light—as more positive role models to girls. In this film, though, she had a plan for making the character more like the type of person she wanted to play. Her character is silly instead of sexy and is stripping because it is her only way to pay for her education. Witherspoon says, "I talked the filmmakers into it being her first night and she isn't a very good stripper."[27] The film, which also stars Paul Rudd, was not a runaway hit but it did help Witherspoon get recognized for her acting.

Witherspoon was developing a fan base. She finished *Overnight Delivery* as *Freeway* was being released. She explains:

> I certainly get the word on the street. People come up to me and tell me what they like and what they don't like. It's all valuable. One of the biggest public reactions I had was on the film "Freeway." Some people have never heard of it but I got such a man-on-the-street response from everyone, like parking garage attendants and 70-year-old women. People just related to that character because she sort of spoke like a real person speaks. It's hard to

Witherspoon with Paul Rudd in a scene from Overnight Delivery. *Reese was reluctant to play a stripper in the film because of her desire to be a role model for young girls.*

relate to movie characters who are so made up and dressed to the nines.[28]

Witherspoon returned to Stanford in the spring of 1996. She also became even more deliberate and careful about the roles she chose. This caused her to turn down many parts and steer clear of particular genres. Rather than make a lot of money quickly, Witherspoon wanted to pick carefully so she could set a foundation for a long career in Hollywood.

In the mid-1990s teen movies, which had been popular in the late 1980s, were making a comeback. The 1980s films had names like *The Breakfast Club*, *Sixteen Candles*, and *Pretty in Pink*, and they featured teen actors playing characters like "the jock," "the homecoming queen," or "the awkward kid." Usually, by the film's end, the characters learn to embrace their differences. For example, in *The Breakfast Club* several different students are forced to serve detention together. Over the course of the day, they become friends and learn that they all have things in common. In *Pretty in Pink*, a poor girl falls for a rich boy and they try to make a relationship work despite the fact that their friends disapprove.

When teen movies began being made in the 1990s, they had lost some of their freshness and originality. Although young actors and actresses had many teen parts to choose from, critics contend that many of these films were not very high quality and did little to further the actors' careers. In addition some actors found themselves getting typecast. They ended up playing the same type of role in the same type of movie again and again.

Witherspoon wanted to avoid this pitfall. She explains: "I . . . purposely avoided a lot of teen-oriented films because I didn't want to be stereotyped as a teen actress in the '90s. . . . I would never limit myself in that way [not take a part she wanted], but I did sort of make a conscious decision not to be identified as a teen actress because I want to have a long career."[29]

It seemed like Witherspoon was in for a long career, too. Yet, she felt like she was caught in the middle of a juggling act. On the one hand, she was making good movies and building an impressive list of credits. On the other, she had school, which she enjoyed and knew was important as well. Witherspoon was stuck—unsure of what to do.

Twilight

But everything seemed to fall into place after she was offered a role in the film *Twilight*, starring Paul Newman, Susan Sarandon, Gene Hackman, and Stockard Channing. Although her role as Mel Ames, the rebellious daughter of two movie stars (played by Hackman and Sarandon), is a supporting one, Witherspoon knew it was a great opportunity. The cast was talented and experienced and Witherspoon was a great admirer of both Newman and Sarandon. There were few chances like this for young actresses.

After working on *Fear* and *Overnight Delivery* (two films she wasn't as proud to have made, because her characters weren't very interesting), Witherspoon had created some rules she wanted to follow for the parts she chose. For example, she did not want to do any gratuitous sex or nude scenes. She wanted to portray characters she admired and that she felt were strong and good role models for girls. She says, "I don't think I ever have a design on [the parts I choose], but I think my personality influences me. I'm

Witherspoon, Paul Newman, and Susan Sarandon appear at the 1998 premiere of Twilight. *Reese was excited to work with such talented veteran actors.*

very ambitious and focused—that's the kind of character I gravitate toward. I also feel a responsibility as an actress to represent women in a way I want to be represented."[30]

Because of the cast, though, Witherspoon bent her rules a little bit for *Twilight*, which required her to do a topless scene.

"Fish Sticks" Newman

Reese Witherspoon was thrilled when she learned she would be working with legendary actor Paul Newman on the film *Twilight*. The Academy Award winner has starred in such classics as *Butch Cassidy and the Sundance Kid*, *The Sting*, and *The Color of Money*, but Witherspoon admires him for more than his acting credits. Through his food line, Newman's Own, which includes salad dressings, popcorn, and pasta sauce, Newman has donated more than $125 million to charities since 1982. And he runs a camp for children with cancer.

Witherspoon was also surprised by how funny and offbeat the actor was. She called the seventy-eight-year-old philanthropist "very cool" and told talk-show host Conan O'Brien, "I loved him. I'm particularly very partial to his food line. So I told him the only thing that's missing from his food line is frozen fish sticks. 'Cause he has frozen everything. And he just thought that was really bizarre, so for the rest of the show I called him fish sticks and everyone else called him fish sticks. . . . Fish Sticks Newman."

While shooting Twilight, *Witherspoon and Paul Newman developed an off-screen friendship.*

When Witherspoon read the movie's script, she decided the top-less scene seemed natural and in character for rebellious Mel. So she agreed to do it. "In fact, the role as written called for full-frontal nudity, and she agreed to do that," the film's director Robert Benton remembers. "The day before we shot the scene, I told her I thought it would be more appropriate to [just have her be topless]."[31]

The scene caused quite a sensation among Witherspoon's fans, who were surprised that she had her top off. Internet sites featuring her topless in movie stills popped up on the Web. But Witherspoon herself was not too concerned. "It's very inconsequential," she said.[32]

Witherspoon loved working with Newman, Sarandon, and Hackman on *Twilight*. She developed a close relationship with Sarandon and the two spent time together both on and off the set. Witherspoon admired Sarandon and her dedication to causes she believed in, such as abortion rights and gun control.

Despite the powerhouse cast, reviews for *Twilight* were mixed, but even criticism of the film did not deter Witherspoon. She had already made up her mind about her future.

Going Hollywood

With a mixture of excitement and reluctance, Witherspoon decided to take an indefinite leave of absence from Stanford. She had completed two semesters but decided she wanted to pursue acting full-time. The hardest part about leaving was breaking the news to her parents. Her family had always been high academic achievers. Witherspoon says, "My dad scored a perfect score on his S.A.T.'s and a perfect score on his MCATs [medical board exams] and graduated at the top of his class from Yale. My mom has five or six degrees."[33] Witherspoon's parents hoped their two children would follow in their footsteps. But neither of them graduated from college.

The Witherspoons were disappointed with their daughter's decision to leave Stanford and they hoped she would one day finish her education. But they supported their daughter. "My parents have instilled in me a work ethic to only do things I feel in my heart," Witherspoon explains.[34] And Reese Witherspoon's heart—and head—were now in acting.

She decided to take a chance, move to Los Angeles, and try to make a career out of what had so far been a lucrative pastime. But Witherspoon was not afraid of taking chances. So after she finished her spring term in 1996, she packed her bags and she and her pet Chihuahua made the move south to Los Angeles.

Chapter 3

Coming into Her Own

Reese Witherspoon was barely out of her teens, but she was thriving professionally. She was on the verge of something big in her personal life as well.

After arriving in Los Angeles, Witherspoon moved into her own apartment and hoped that she had made the right decision in giving up college for acting. It soon became clear that she had. Over the next two years, she made three different films. "The ball just started rolling," Witherspoon says. "The roles kept getting better and better, and that's when I realized I could make a career out of this."[35]

Life in Los Angeles

Initially, not everyone thought Witherspoon was going to be a star. Witherspoon recalled one incident that had her wondering if she had made a mistake by moving to Los Angeles. "When I first moved to Los Angeles, I went to see a doctor and he said, 'Reese Witherspoon? Well, there's a name you'll never see in lights.'"[36] Little did that doctor know just how many movies Witherspoon would someday headline.

In the meantime, Witherspoon was getting adjusted to life in Los Angeles. Northern California (where Stanford was located) had been very different from Nashville; and Southern California was even more of a culture shock. She could not believe how many kids her age were driving around in expensive cars like Porsches and BMWs. She was also surprised by the lack of manners people had. Witherspoon explains: "When I first got here, I was surprised that people didn't say 'please' and 'thank you' or call other people 'ma'am' and 'sir.' I know that seems naive, but I grew up with a really polite, conservative structure."[37] Witherspoon, however, makes it a point not to give up her southern ways. She still addresses people politely and always sends thank-you notes and cards or gifts for birthdays and special occasions.

Witherspoon also decided not to give in to Hollywood pressures and temptations. Even though she was making enough money to live luxuriously, she had a small apartment and was careful about what she spent. Witherspoon was determined not to get caught up in what she had or what she looked like. She says:

> I certainly think the longer you can keep your values and your morality intact, and keep your head on your shoulders about what is important at the end of the day, you can get the most out of this business and really emerge with something wonderful. . . . I think it's important to start realizing at a young age that your body is just a vessel for who you are as a person. And until you work on what you give back to the world, it doesn't matter what you look like on the outside.[38]

It helps, too, that Witherspoon has never seen herself as a sexy Hollywood star, so she never acts the part. Even though many people have called her beautiful, Witherspoon would not be one of the first to say so. The five-foot-two-inch natural blond does not think too much about hair and makeup. And she has never been wary of playing down her looks for a role. "This actress came up to me and said, 'What I really like about you is you're not afraid to be ugly,'" Witherspoon told a reporter in 2002. "And you know what? She was kind of right—I really don't care. Someone once asked me what my best side is. I'm like, 'I don't know—the front?'"[39]

Finding Love

It is that refreshing modesty that earns Witherspoon many friends. Even though she had been in Los Angeles for less than a year, more than three hundred people showed up to celebrate Witherspoon's twenty-first birthday at a party held for her at a nightclub in downtown Los Angeles. Witherspoon's family even made the trip from Nashville to attend the event.

Ryan Phillippe

Matthew Ryan Phillippe was born on September 10, 1974, in New Castle, Delaware, a town thirty miles outside of Philadelphia. He has three older sisters, Kirsten, Lindsay, and Katelyn. Phillippe's father, Richard, is a chemical technician for DuPont and his mother, Susan, ran a day-care center out of their home.

Phillippe moved to New York City after he graduated from high school. The seventeen-year-old wanted to be an actor but found it hard to break into the business at first. He modeled and took part-time jobs to support himself, including working at a video store and selling crabs and seafood. He landed his first acting job playing a gay teen (the first ever portrayed on television) on the ABC soap opera *One Life to Live*.

After living and working in New York City for a couple of years, Phillippe moved to Los Angeles to work in film. There, he met fellow struggling actors Seth Green and Breckin Meyer. The three became best friends and later, after their individual successes, even started their own production company.

In 1995 Phillippe got his big break after being cast in a TV movie called *Deadly Invasion: The Killer Bee Nightmare*. Director Ridley Scott

noticed the talented twenty-year-old and cast him in his feature film *White Squall*. Since *White Squall*, Phillippe has not stopped working. He has starred in more than twenty films including *54*, *Playing by Heart*, and *I Know What You Did Last Summer*.

Ryan Phillippe in a scene from 54, one of more than twenty films in which the talented young actor has starred.

One of the well-wishers present that night was a young actor named Ryan Phillippe, who had starred in the film *White Squall*. The twenty-two-year-old later admitted that he had come to the party for the free beer. But after a mutual friend introduced Phillippe and Witherspoon, the two did not leave each other's sides for the rest of the night. Witherspoon says, "When we met, we both realized right away that we wanted to spend our lives together; we were really well matched. I've always believed that you just know who your partner in life is when you meet. I knew with Ryan."[40]

The two spent most of the night talking and Witherspoon learned that Phillippe had to leave for North Carolina the next morning to begin shooting the film *I Know What You Did Last Summer*. Although Witherspoon was disappointed that Phillippe was going to be out of town for three months, the two exchanged addresses and phone numbers and promised to stay in touch. Witherspoon remembers:

> He seemed like this really nice guy, just really sweet and easy to get along with. He wasn't trying to put on a fake "I'm a cool actor guy" front. My dad and brother were there, and Ryan was like, "Oh, I want to meet them and say hi!" He was really polite and respectful. The next day he left town to shoot *I Know What You Did Last Summer*. We wrote each other letters and called each other a lot. He sent me his favorite books and I sent him mine, *The End of the Affair*. It was really cool because he was into reading and was so smart.[41]

Although the two had spent only a few hours together, they were falling in love. Phillippe took great care in drafting his letters to Witherspoon. "I would make the letters sound very Edith Wharton [the romantic, turn-of-the-century author]," he later told a reporter. "Kind of like, 'My love—how are you doing?' We'd never even kissed. The attraction was mental—we were interested in each other in the most genuine way."[42]

While Ryan was both mentally and physically attracted to Witherspoon, there was something even more intriguing about their relationship. Phillippe says, "We would have conversations on the phone before we even had our first date. We would cover every subject imaginable. She would challenge me, and I would challenge her. What struck me most about her was her mind, although she was also adorable and sexy. I was struck by her individuality—a self-possessed woman with her own ideas about things."[43] Witherspoon has her own idea about why her relationship with Phillippe worked. "It wasn't the typical courtship," she admits. "I was definitely the aggressor. I had a really good instinct about the kind of person he was, and it turned out I was right."[44]

The couple finally had their first date two months into their relationship. Even though Witherspoon was in California shooting the film *Pleasantville* and Phillippe was in North Carolina, she decided they had been apart long enough. Witherspoon explains:

> I had like three days off work. I was talking to my [*Pleasantville*] costar Tobey Maguire, I was like, "I don't know what to do, Ryan wants me to come out there, I'm so conflicted." And Tobey was like, "You know what Reese? I've heard you talk about him. I can tell how crazy you are about him. And you should totally do it. Because if some girl did that for me, it would totally make my lifetime." . . . And I walked off the plane and just totally freaked out. I was like "Oh, my God, I don't even know you."[45]

Phillippe understood why Witherspoon was not at ease with the situation. She did not really know him that well, and she had just taken the risk of traveling to see him, hoping it would work out when they were face to face. Phillippe said, "You know, I had three bedrooms and all this stuff. I wasn't going to assume anything. Then she shows up and looks at me and the color runs out of her face. She had this look of fear in her eyes. And she was like, 'I shouldn't have come alone. I have to go call my mother.' She'd just gotten off the plane."[46]

Luckily, Witherspoon's mother told her the same thing Maguire had—and what Witherspoon knew in her heart but needed to hear. She was definitely in love with Phillippe. Within a few months, the two were living together in a little green house in Beverly Hills.

Pleasantville

While she was falling in love, Witherspoon was also working on *Pleasantville*, a unique film about a suburban 1990s brother and sister who get sucked into the television-series lives of a seemingly perfect but cardboard 1950s family. Most of the film is in black and white, but colors appear as the 1950s characters are introduced to real feelings and emotions by the brother-sister pair.

The movie's message is that things are not always how they appear. It is a theme Witherspoon liked. The first glimpse viewers get of the 1950s town of Pleasantville is, she explains,

> this perfect, idyllic setting with picket fences and beautiful houses and nice, white families. But as the movie progresses, you start to see this undercurrent of everything that was "underneath" [life in] the Fifties. Especially Fifties television turmoil and hate and discomfort and distress,

Tobey Maguire and Witherspoon in a scene from Pleasantville. *Critics applauded both the film and Witherspoon's outstanding performance.*

and I think people will really be talking about how this movie sort of represents the juxtaposition between what was on television in the Fifties and what was really happening in the Fifties.[47]

The film's two young stars, Witherspoon and Tobey Maguire, spent a lot of time together in the months before filming and soon became very close. The two struck up a friendship that continues today, and Maguire has nothing but praise for his costar. He says: "To be that talented, to be such an interesting human being, and to make such smart decisions in your career—it's pretty amazing and pretty rare."[48]

But Maguire was not the only fan Witherspoon had on the set. *Pleasantville*'s writer and director Gary Ross was amazed by her. "Witherspoon is like this Mighty Mite, this little cartoon hero," he says. "She reminds me of great comedic actresses of another time: Carole Lombard, Rosalind Russell, even Judy Holliday."[49]

When the movie was released in 1998, critics also praised *Pleasantville* for its originality and for the performances of its stars. Witherspoon was singled out. Charles Taylor of Salon.com writes, "With her face set hard and mean . . . Witherspoon gives the movie a jolt of surly contempt that keeps it going through the clumsy and sluggish scenes establishing the premise."[50] *Pleasantville* was also on many critics' top-ten lists for the year, and Roger Ebert of the *Chicago Sun-Times* gave it four stars. For her outstanding work in the movie, Witherspoon was awarded the Movieline Young Hollywood Award for Breakthrough Performance by a Female.

Election

Witherspoon followed her lauded performance in *Pleasantville* with her most acclaimed to date, a role in the film *Election*. The movie tells the story of an overly ambitious high school student named Tracy Flick. Tracy is running unopposed as student council president until Mr. McAllister, a popular teacher and the student government adviser (who is also experiencing a premature midlife crisis), decides that overachieving Tracy needs some competition. He

Witherspoon gives out campaign cupcakes in a scene from Election. *Her work in the movie won her very high critical acclaim.*

recruits ex-jock Paul Metzler to run against her—and that is when the sparks begin to fly.

Witherspoon's agent gave her the *Election* script in 1997. When Witherspoon read the script she knew she had to play Tracy Flick. She loved the story. She says, "I first read this script immediately after I finished 'Pleasantville' and it was so completely different that I couldn't resist it. I also had a great idea about how to play the character. I knew exactly what she sounded like, I knew exactly what she looked like. I knew how she walked, how she even held her jaw. I knew exactly who she was."[51]

All Witherspoon had to do was convince director Alexander Payne that the role should be hers. Payne had seen Witherspoon in *The Man in the Moon* and had been impressed with her work even then. He knew she was a competent actress. But he was not prepared for the headstrong woman who walked through his door that day. When Payne asked her why she wanted the role,

Witherspoon replied, "There's just nobody better for this part than me. I deliver the goods."[52]

Payne could not argue with that. He offered her the role. And he found that Witherspoon was true to her word. "She's the real McCoy. She concocted that voice, that walk, the way Tracy pogos in the hallway when she thinks she's won [the election]," Payne says.[53]

Witherspoon drew inspiration for her characterization of Tracy Flick from two sources. The first was some extremely driven people she knew at Stanford who were always working at academics and never socialized. The second was a girl she knew in junior high school. Of that girl, Witherspoon told a reporter: "She was so perfect. Had all the boyfriends and [was] the smartest girl in school. And she was rude to me! This is my little revenge. I'm doing her in this. Certain elements [are her], and I wore my hair the way she did."[54]

Although the film was a satire and meant to be funny, Witherspoon was concerned that Tracy not become a caricature. She wanted the character to be taken seriously so she went to

Witherspoon's Favorite Things

Reese Witherspoon is a busy actress, but she also enjoys relaxing and enjoying some of her favorite music, books, movies, and snacks. She revealed some of her favorites in the article "17 Minutes with Reese" by Geri Richter Campbell of *Seventeen* magazine:

Favorite CD: I just borrow Ryan's albums because he has better taste in music than I do. My favorite CD would have to be either Lauryn Hill's *The Miseducation of Lauryn Hill* or Jay Z's *MTV Unplugged* CD. I also like Fiona Apple.

Favorite Book: I'm reading *The Lovely Bones* by Alice Sebold right now. I'm also reading *Vanity Fair* by William Thackeray. And I just reread *The Diary of Anne Frank*, which is always moving. I'm also reading *The Catcher in the Rye* this summer because I saw it on the summer reading list at the bookstore and I got all excited to do summer reading again.

Favorite Movie: I have lots of favorite movies, but whenever I'm really in a bad mood I watch *Overboard*. It's a laugh a minute.

Favorite Food: Lately, I can't get enough of those chocolate-dipped coconut ice pops. They're so good. Fruit-A-Freeze bars—yum, they are delicious. Perfect snack.

Payne for advice on how to play it straight. "I would give her advice about that, [which] just rippled through her whole performance," Payne raves. "It was like watching bacteria replicating in a petri dish—she's so smart."[55]

Although Witherspoon enjoyed making *Election*, some things about filming were difficult. She was faced with months away from Phillippe, whom she missed terribly, and a very cold fall in Nebraska, where the film was shot. This was hard on a girl used to warm Southern California.

"She's a Dynamo"

In addition to missing Phillippe and being cold, Witherspoon also became a student again after Payne suggested that she enroll in a local high school and pretend to be a transfer student. The experience was an eye-opening one for the actress. She explains:

> It was really interesting because I was escorted by a girl very much like my character—president of the student council, captain of the volleyball team, and head cheerleader—a total overachiever. The experience helped me get back in the mind-set of teenagers and empathize with their problems. . . . I was amazed at how busy students are now, running around at a hectic pace doing all these different activities. The girls wake up very early to do their hair and makeup to make sure they look perfect. Going back to school was always kind of a vacation for me, but these kids are having high school careers.[56]

Witherspoon spent two weeks attending school and conducting research. But the students discovered who she was in just two days. She claimed that by the second day the students had figured out who she was and were throwing food at her in the cafeteria for fun.

Despite the flying food, Witherspoon says researching and making *Election* was a great experience for her. She had tremendous respect for Payne and for her costar, Matthew Broderick, who played Mr. McAllister. Witherspoon was a huge fan of the actor and admitted to having a little crush on him when she was growing up. Broderick was equally enthusiastic about working

TRACY FLICK
FOR PRESIDENT!
SIGN UP FOR
TOMORROW
TODAY!

Matthew Broderick appears in a scene with Witherspoon in Election.
*Reese enjoyed working with Broderick, an actor for whom she had
long-standing respect.*

with Witherspoon. "She's a dynamo—this small package filled
with power."[57]

Moviegoers and critics were won over by Witherspoon as well.
Roger Ebert of the *Chicago Sun-Times* says, "[Witherspoon] hits her
full stride in 'Election' as an aggressive, manipulative vixen who
informs a teacher she hopes they can work together 'harmoniously'
in the coming school year."[58]

Witherspoon received many nominations and awards for her
work, including a Golden Globe nomination for Best Performance
by an Actress in a Musical or Comedy and Best Actress awards
from the Online Critics Society and National Society of Film Critics.

Election was filmed in the fall of 1997. But it was not released
until the spring of 1999, just after the next movie Witherspoon
made—*Cruel Intentions.*

Working with Ryan

With the role of virginal Annette Hargrove in *Cruel Intentions,* an
updated version of the film *Dangerous Liaisons,* Witherspoon did
a complete turnaround from her last two parts. The film focuses
on Katherine (played by Sarah Michelle Gellar) and Sebastian
(played by Ryan Phillippe), a rich and ruthless stepsister and step-
brother who make a bet over whether or not Sebastian can sleep

with the admittedly chaste Annette (played by Witherspoon). "It's set in modern-day New York with teenage socialites, and it's biting and dark and mean—but it has a wonderful emotional heart," Witherspoon says.[59]

At first, though, Witherspoon was not sure she wanted to take the role. She was tired and thought she needed a break before taking on another project. She explains:

> I had just finished four movies in a row and was really tired. I didn't want to hear the word movie, much less make a movie. But Ryan convinced me to read it, and then I met Roger [Kumble, the writer-director] and decided it was something I wasn't going to pass up. But we completely rewrote my character Annette before shooting. In the orig-

A publicity shot for the movie Cruel Intentions *shows the film's stars (from back to front) Sarah Michelle Gellar, Ryan Phillippe, Reese Witherspoon, and Selma Blair.*

inal script she was more like the *Dangerous Liaisons* character, timid and shy, and it didn't make sense to me. She'd be devoured by these predatory people! I made her an intellectual, a woman wedded to her principles, and it made her seem more attainable in a different way.[60]

Witherspoon had another reason for taking the part. She would be starring opposite boyfriend Ryan Phillippe. After being apart for so many months, it was nice for the two to be together all day during the six-week shoot in New York and Los Angeles and then come home and discuss their characters and the filming. The couple had been together for more than a year and were still blissfully in love. This sometimes made certain aspects of playing their characters very difficult. In a pivotal scene in the film, Annette and Sebastian have a fight and break up. Witherspoon and Phillippe did so many takes of the scene, they eventually started ad-libbing, or making up some of their lines. Some of Phillippe's were so hurtful that Witherspoon became enraged and slapped him. The director loved the addition, but Phillippe was shaken. Afterward, he admitted he threw up because he was so upset.

But everything else about filming was great for the pair. They enjoyed working with the young cast that included Gellar and Selma Blair. Witherspoon and Blair struck up a friendship (they later starred in *Legally Blonde* together). Blair was impressed with Witherspoon's professionalism and the way she would stand up for herself and others on the set. Blair says, "There were times on the set where I might have compromised something of myself and she'd say in the nicest possible way, 'You're worth more than that.'"[61]

This was not a new occurrence for Witherspoon, who often found herself defending fellow actors. Witherspoon explains why she stands up for other actors: "I think a lot of people in this industry want to shine and want other people to be dull, but I think there's plenty of room for all of us. And if that's not true, I'll just go do something else."[62]

Reviews for *Cruel Intentions* were mixed, but the film gave Witherspoon a name among teens and young adults who went to see it. She was being recognized more by young fans both as an actress and as heartthrob Ryan Phillippe's girlfriend. Witherspoon was about to become much more than just Phillippe's girlfriend, though. In December 1998 they got engaged, and in March 1999, just before *Cruel Intentions* was released in theaters, the couple announced they were expecting a baby. Witherspoon and Phillippe were going to be parents and they were thrilled.

Chapter 4

Putting Family First

ALTHOUGH SHE WAS just twenty-two and her career was starting to take off, Reese Witherspoon welcomed having a baby. She knew she had found her partner in Ryan Phillippe and that he would make a great dad. The couple saw their lives as lucky even though the pregnancy was unplanned. Phillippe explains, "We found out. It just seemed like a blessing. We'd been together two years. You know, this business does mature you pretty quickly. It made sense to us. I can handle it. I have the energy, we have the patience, we have the money. It just felt like something I shouldn't question, and she shouldn't question. We thought about it for a while and then it was . . . apparent."[63]

The couple soon decided to get married. Phillippe proposed to Witherspoon after making her favorite breakfast—waffles with strawberries and whipped cream—and serving it to her in bed. Witherspoon quickly accepted. Reese Witherspoon was getting ready for some pretty big new roles—wife and mother—but she was ready for the challenges that lay ahead.

The Wedding

One of the first challenges Witherspoon faced was telling her family that she was getting married and that she was pregnant. In her family, babies came after marriage and not before. Witherspoon decided that the easiest way to break the news was just to come right out with it. The Witherspoons were surprised but supportive. And they were excited to welcome a new member into the family.

Witherspoon was also worried about how her friends from high school would react to the news. They also believed in getting married before starting a family but proved supportive. Witherspoon says her best friend was shocked, "but she said wonderful things to me. She said, 'I think you of all people are ready for this.' That made me feel much better about things. The fact that people really believe in you is wonderful."[64]

The next challenge the couple faced was finding a place to live. Prior to learning that Witherspoon was pregnant, she and Phillippe had been looking for an apartment together in New York City. But they quickly abandoned the idea after they found out they were expecting. Witherspoon thought it would be too much of an adjustment moving away from their friends to a new and unfamiliar city. So, they stayed in their house in Beverly Hills and started making plans for both a wedding and a baby.

Witherspoon spent the next few months planning the wedding. It was a challenge. She was very busy with doctor's ap-

Reese's Surprise Pregnancy

Reese Witherspoon was surprised to find out she was going to become a mother at age twenty-three. But it was a surprise she welcomed because she believed it was meant to be. She told Barry Koltnow of the *Orange County Register:*

Yes, it [the pregnancy] was a surprise, but I don't believe in accidents. Something like this chooses you. I panicked initially but ultimately came to realize that no movie job was as big as the job I'm facing now. This has given me such an incredible sense of purpose. . . . Once that initial panic faded, a kind of bliss came over me. I want to continue acting, and I want to achieve a certain measure of success, but what good is success if you have no one to share it with?

A pregnant Reese appears alongside husband Ryan Phillippe at a 1999 Oscar party.

pointments and making movies. In addition, Witherspoon said, "It is hard to plan a nice, big southern wedding on the spur of the moment. I am trying not to pressure myself into doing it."[65] It was difficult, too, for her to decide where the wedding should take place since her family and Ryan Phillippe's family lived hundreds of miles apart. In the end, the couple chose to have a casual, comfortable ceremony in Charleston, South Carolina, because it was a good halfway point between the Witherspoons' home in Nashville and the Phillippes' in Wilmington, Delaware.

On June 5, 1999, Witherspoon and Phillippe were married on a farm in Charleston. They exchanged vows on a riverbank under a weeping willow tree. It was very hot and the bride was almost seven months pregnant, but the wedding went just the way Witherspoon had planned. She even had the traditional something old (vintage fabric appliquéd on her dress), something new (her white lace wedding dress), something borrowed (her mother's earrings), and something blue (her bouquet was blue flowers). A gospel choir sang the Etta James classic "At Last," after the couple was pronounced husband and wife. Only a small crowd of family and friends were invited to the ceremony. Witherspoon and Phillippe kept it low-key and private.

More Movies

After the wedding Witherspoon went back to work. She was no longer filming movies, but she had four films being released in 1999 (*Cruel Intentions, Election, Best Laid Plans,* and *American Psycho*). She had to go to the films' premieres and after-parties and give numerous interviews about her roles.

In the independent film *Best Laid Plans*, Witherspoon plays a girl named Lissa who hatches a plot with her boyfriend Nick to frame his rich friend for rape. Although the film was not seen by many people, reviews for *Best Laid Plans* were generally positive. James Berardinelli of ReelViews says, "Both [actor] Alessandro Nivola and Reese Witherspoon offer strong portrayals of two lovers who struggle with their consciences even though they are out of options. Witherspoon, who with every new performance is growing into an actress of great depth and range, is especially impressive."[66]

Witherspoon and Alessandro Nivola appear in a scene from Best Laid Plans, *an independent film which firmly established Reese's credibility as a serious actress.*

Witherspoon's last film of 1999, *American Psycho*, was filmed in the early months of her pregnancy. Witherspoon was excited about her small role in the film about a yuppie serial killer named Patrick Bateman. She plays his socialite fiancée, Evelyn. The film was controversial because there was a lot of violence, and several people close to Witherspoon advised her against appearing in it. But in the end, she decided to take a chance. Witherspoon explains:

> Obviously, I had to be sure about this. I read the book and had a long discussion with [director] Mary Harron, and we had a sort of similar view about the film. To me, the movie is a dark satire of a male response to the sexual liberation of women in the early '80s. That women didn't need men was a new thing for these young men who were doing everything possible to be impressive and wearing these designer shoes and having these wonderful apartments and spending this money and women just didn't

[care]. The story is about this man who responds to inadequacies with the only control he has in his life, which is to put women in these horrible, compromising positions. Mary has this wonderful black tone in mind, and she really knows what she's talking about. I really think she's going to pull it off.[67]

Another reason Witherspoon took the part was the chance to work with Christian Bale, the actor playing Patrick Bateman. Witherspoon was a big fan of the actor. She says, "I've seen pretty much all of his work since *Empire of the Sun* and I was so excited to work with him. He's a really wonderful actor who makes very smart decisions and doesn't ever compromise his integrity."[68]

Although Witherspoon enjoyed the cast and crew and had fun during filming, *American Psycho* failed to impress critics and audiences who did not feel the movie had the same edge as the book. However, by the time it was released, Witherspoon was too happy—and busy with her new baby—to care.

Getting Ready for Baby

In the weeks leading up her baby's arrival, Witherspoon grew excited about her new role of mother and explained that she and her husband were looking forward to the changes their baby would bring to their lives. "I'm very excited about the baby. I realize no movie can ever be as important as the process and journey we're going though now," she said during her pregnancy. "I think it's very easy to take time in your life to work on your career, but it's harder to take time to work on the quality of your life. But that's sort of what we plan on doing for the next year."[69]

Life was hectic in the weeks before the baby was born. In order to decorate and buy gender-appropriate baby things, Phillippe and Witherspoon decided that they wanted to find out the baby's sex. When Witherspoon was twenty weeks along, her doctor did an ultrasound. Witherspoon and Phillippe discovered they would be painting in pink. Witherspoon said: "I was surprised when the ultrasound revealed that I was having a girl; I was convinced I was having a boy. And I was completely confounded by the fact that I wasn't in control of the situation—that

I was being introduced to a different individual coming into my life."[70]

Fortunately for Witherspoon, her new individual was pretty cooperative. The mother-to-be did not have any morning sickness and felt healthy throughout the nine months of her pregnancy. Like many pregnant women, she did have some strange cravings, though. Witherspoon wanted anything grape flavored as well as root beer and seafood. And she joked about having to have an entire supermarket in the refrigerator so that she could whip up anything she felt like eating whenever she wanted it.

During her pregnancy, Witherspoon also experienced mood swings. She had not been expecting these and got some helpful advice from her doctor about how to deal with them. She explains:

> During my pregnancy I was so hormonal, especially in the last three weeks. There's that song from the movie Dumbo, "Baby of Mine," which the mother elephant sings to her baby from jail. Every time I would think of that song, which was often, I burst into tears. All the crying was exhausting. But I loved visiting my OB/GYN [obstetrician/gynecologist, a doctor who delivers babies]. She was so easygoing and patient with me. The most important piece of advice I got was to be positive. To think, "Yes, I can have this baby." Any positive thought will help. Saying "NO, NO, NO," doesn't help anybody in the delivery room.[71]

Despite the emotional roller coaster, Witherspoon enjoyed being pregnant. And the expectant father did not seem to mind his wife's fluctuating hormones. Phillippe bought Witherspoon flowers and cookies for Mother's Day. And just before the baby's arrival, the pair had fun shopping for pink baby clothes and talking to their unborn daughter.

Starring Ava Elizabeth

On September 9, 1999, a very pregnant Witherspoon was shopping in Beverly Hills when she went into labor. Seven-pound Ava Elizabeth Phillippe was born later that day. Ava was named after

Reese visits with her husband Ryan Phillippe and daughter Ava on the set of Legally Blonde. *Despite her demanding acting career, Reese feels parenting is her most important job.*

both Phillippe's grandmother, Eva, and actress Ava Gardner, whom Phillippe admires.

Witherspoon remembers being nervous about holding her own daughter at first because she had never held an infant before. Luckily, Witherspoon's mother, Betty, came to help take care of the baby for the first several months of Ava's life. Witherspoon grew to appreciate her mother even more after she became one herself. She came to realize all of the work that is involved in raising children. It was the biggest job she had ever had—and the most time-consuming.

Luckily, Phillippe also had some practical experience with babies and toddlers. Witherspoon explains: "Ryan's mom provided day care in their house when he was little. He knows how to negotiate a child out of a temper tantrum like you wouldn't believe. He potty-trained Ava all by himself. He's a terrific father. I'm always amazed by him."[72]

While Phillippe did not seem to have any trouble accepting and loving his new parenting role, Witherspoon struggled with being a new mother at first. Although she loved Ava, she knew her life would never be the same and she was also saddened by this fact. She admits, "It was hard. I was trying to understand my new position as a woman and what it all meant. I went through a long period when I was really depressed and I couldn't figure out why. When you're living your life, sometimes it's hard to see how wonderful it is. I finally realized I had this wonderful guy and child, and I wasn't going to throw it away by being miserable."[73]

Witherspoon says motherhood has taught her many lessons. In addition to appreciating her own mother more, Witherspoon says she has a better sense of humor and takes herself less seriously than she did before she had Ava. In motherhood, Witherspoon has also discovered a source of happiness and contentment that she never knew existed until after Ava's birth. She explains, "As a single woman, there's a constant pressure to find a man or figure out where you fit in the workplace. But with motherhood, there's this wonderful sense that I could lose my job and still raise a child and feel completely fulfilled."[74]

The Challenges of Parenting

Reese Witherspoon found that parenting had its challenges and she had to fight to overcome them. She says in an E!Online interview:

Nobody told me about the sleep deprivation. Ava was waking up several times a night for the the first five months, and I just remember standing over her crib thinking, Please go to sleep! Please go to sleep! That was a challenge. But it's great having something in your life that is really grounding, something that gives you focus. So much of what we deal with is artificial, and a child is a dose of reality. . . . Parenthood is an exercise in tolerance and patience. It's a challenge, but you have to know other people have gone through it, too. That's one of the most important things— talk. Talk to other women and have your husband talk to other dads. It's so important to have friends to rely on, even if they're not people you know. I met a lot of people in a parenting support group.

The End of Maternity Leave

Despite feeling fulfilled with her personal life, after a few months at home, Witherspoon was anxious to get back to work. She was not ready to commit to long hours over several months away from Ava, though. The solution was a guest appearance on the sitcom *Friends*. Witherspoon had gotten hooked on the show during her pregnancy and was excited to meet the cast.

She appeared on two episodes as Rachel's spoiled little sister Jill. The shows were filmed in December 1999 and aired in February 2000. Phillippe and the baby accompanied Witherspoon to the set, and the cast and crew enjoyed playing with Ava.

Although she had fun rehearsing and getting to know the other actors, Witherspoon admitted she had stage fright during shooting. She had never performed in front of a live audience. "It's a live audience and I had never done anything in front of a live audience. And there's nothing worse than, like, telling a joke and it totally bricks [bombs] and nobody laughs," she says.[75]

Still, Witherspoon had fun playing Jill, a shopaholic with no career or aspirations. In addition to the role, Witherspoon enjoyed the experience because she was impressed by the cast. "I had a great time guest starring on *Friends*," she said. "The cast is so talented, they make what they do every day seem effortless. But I realized after being on the show how incredibly hard each one of them works every day. I was very impressed with their comic timing and the way they work so well with each other."[76]

With her first role after the baby was born now under her belt, Witherspoon started reading movie scripts again. She wanted to play women Ava could admire one day—and Witherspoon hoped that would help Ava admire and respect her too. She says:

> When I had a child, it really changed my whole perspective on my career and on my life. It turns your whole world upside down because you're willing to sacrifice anything for this little person. It changed my personality a lot—you take inventory on yourself and realize, "Okay, that's kind of a quality I would never want her to emulate." I was very young [twenty-three] when I had her, and she really helped me to grow up, become more mature,

Witherspoon appears in a scene with Jennifer Aniston on the television show Friends. *Her guest role on the show allowed her to try out a new character.*

more of the kind of woman I would want my daughter to be. I think it's important not to make decisions that you wouldn't want your kids to make. It's also important to me, for her sake, to help advance the role of women in this industry, to make sure the female voice is strong.[77]

Witherspoon's next role was one she was sure her daughter would want to see. She lent her voice to the animated version of the classic children's book *The Trumpet of the Swan*. Witherspoon had such a good time making the children's film, she also played an animated character on the FOX series *King of the Hill*. Like her guest role on *Friends*, Witherspoon's experience providing voices was new and different, but one she enjoyed.

Next, Witherspoon had a small role as Adam Sandler's mother in the comedy *Little Nicky*. Witherspoon was pleased with the filming schedule and loved working with funnyman Sandler. He made her laugh on the set, and her part was small enough that she was always home for dinner.

Raising Ava

Witherspoon may be a movie star but she is also like most other mothers. Her greatest joys are no longer professional, but personal. She likes spending time at home with Ryan and Ava. The family makes dinner, bakes together, and plays with their dogs, an English bulldog named Frank Sinatra and a Chihuahua named Chi Chi. They also dine together every Sunday morning at Denny's—just like "regular" people. Witherspoon says, "My reality check comes at the end of the day when I go home, make dinner and play with Ava. Ryan and I don't do the 'glamour couple' thing. We save the clothes and hair and makeup for work. The fun times for us are at home with our daughter and two dogs. And going to

Reese shares a lighthearted moment with her husband at a Los Angeles Lakers' basketball game. The couple maintains a down-to-earth lifestyle despite their fame.

Nashville to see my parents always reminds me that there are lots of other things going on in the world besides movies."[78]

The couple have also made their home kid-friendly. Witherspoon and Phillippe let Ava draw on the walls with washable markers and have inexpensive furniture in case their daughter ruins it. Witherspoon explains, "People try to sell us expensive stuff and I just think, Can a kid spill on it? What about grape juice? Ryan and I looked at these ludicrously expensive carpets the other day. They were gorgeous but Ryan told me, 'We always said we wanted a house that our kids could destroy.' And he was so right."[79]

Witherspoon loves watching Ava grow, and the two spend a lot of time together. Witherspoon drives her daughter to preschool in the mornings and takes her to Mommy and Me classes where they sing and dance. Ava has also begun to develop her own personality, one that is both different from and similar to her mother's. Unlike Witherspoon, who was a tomboy, Ava does not like to get dirty. But like her mother, Ava loves to read books. Witherspoon told a reporter: "I discovered that the biggest surprise about motherhood is that your children are nothing like you in particular. They might adopt certain aspects of your personality or say certain things similar to you because they hear you, but they're individuals. They just completely surprise you everyday."[80]

While Ava is busy surprising her parents, Witherspoon and Ryan Phillippe work hard at trying to make sure she is raised with the right values. Witherspoon claims she would love to move back to Nashville some day, far away from Hollywood and its emphasis on material possessions. Witherspoon's friend, Jessica Teich, explains, "She wants to give her child the kind of upbringing she had and knows she's going to have to work hard to achieve that."[81]

But Witherspoon admits that it is a struggle to pass on certain values to a child who is growing up surrounded by so much material wealth. "You hear that the kid next door has a fire truck and you're like, 'A real fire truck?' 'Yeah, a real one.' It's about what you instill in your children. You have to fight a little more."[82]

In addition to fighting to teach Ava the value of a dollar, Witherspoon is also working to make sure that Ava values herself. Witherspoon wants Ava to believe she can be anything she wants to be (as Witherspoon is) and knows that women are valu-

Independent Ava

Reese Witherspoon and Ryan Phillippe are raising their daughter to be very independent. This is a good thing for Ava, but hard on Witherspoon who claims that she misses her daughter more than Ava misses her. Witherspoon told Josh Rottenberg of *InStyle* magazine: "The other day she said to me, 'Mommy, when I start school, I'm not going to need you anymore.' It was like my heart was ripped out of my body—but you have to foster that individuality and respect it and nurture it."

able for more than just the way they look. So, instead of buying Ava plain Barbie dolls, Witherspoon bought her several President of the United States Barbies to satisfy her daughter's desire for Barbie as well as her own wish that Ava see the doll as more than just pretty.

Witherspoon had decided also that her next film role would be about a beautiful girl who was more than she appeared. That role was as Elle Woods in a comedy called *Legally Blonde*. And it would make her a certified star.

Chapter 5

Commercial Success

Prior to making *Legally Blonde*, Reese Witherspoon had more critics than moviegoers as fans. She had made many acclaimed films but had yet to have a big blockbuster to make her a movie star. Although Witherspoon was not intentionally looking to make a commercial success, she found one with *Legally Blonde*. "It's just good luck really," she says. "Just fortune. You gamble every time you make a movie."[83]

Blondes Have More Fun

The comedy seemed very silly and light-hearted, but Witherspoon loved its message: Do not judge a book (or in this case, a blonde) by its (or her) cover. "I think it has a great message about believing in yourself, following your dreams and not being subservient in a relationship or to other people's judgments of you," Witherspoon says. "I felt it was sort of a responsibility to start speaking to my young female fans because they are so easily influenced."[84]

Elle Woods, Witherspoon's character in *Legally Blonde*, is a Southern California sorority girl who loves to shop, get her nails done, and dine at expensive restaurants with her boyfriend, Warner Huntington III. One night at dinner, though, Warner breaks up with Elle. Warner, who is headed for Harvard Law School in the fall, thinks she is not smart enough for him to marry. Determined to prove him wrong, Elle gets into Harvard Law as well and causes a sensation once enrolled.

To research the role, Witherspoon spent time with University of Southern California (USC) sorority girls and got into playing the part. She says:

I went to the University of Southern California and hung out in the sorority houses, went to meetings, and really got to know the girls. I went to law school for a few days and did research in Neiman Marcus watching the ladies have lunch and how they walked. I think all of those behavior studies are really important because you learn how people behave toward each other. . . . Once you get into it, and really studied these women at USC, I think you totally understand why they're so positive and upbeat, it's just sort of the mentality they have, a sort of learned cultural response.[85]

In addition to her liking the character and the film's message, the movie was being filmed in Southern California. So Witherspoon could be home with her husband and daughter each night. Her good friend Selma Blair was also in the film, playing a snooty brunette Elle shows up.

Challenges of *Legally Blonde*

Once Witherspoon got into the head of her character, her work had only just begun. There were other challenges she faced in

Witherspoon in a scene from the movie Legally Blonde. *Reese chose to do the movie because of its atypical and positive portrayal of a seemingly superficial sorority girl.*

playing Elle. First, she had to work on getting into her outfits. Witherspoon had sixty costume changes in the movie, and she was overwhelmed with three weeks of fittings.

In addition, Witherspoon was working out every day to get back into shape and fit into her costumes. Witherspoon had gained forty-two pounds while she was pregnant and she had to be in a bikini for the film. So MGM, the company making the movie hired a personal trainer who had her running and doing yoga. Witherspoon, who claims she was never very athletic, discovered she liked pushing her body to do new things. She had fun working out and found it was a good way to relieve stress.

Witherspoon faced other challenges in playing the ever positive Elle. The workdays were long, sometimes lasting nineteen hours, and there were fifty-two days of filming. Because Witherspoon was the star of the film, she was on the set every day. It was an exhausting schedule for a new mother. Witherspoon explains, "It was definitely a challenge to be perky all the time, especially when you have a 5 a.m. call and you've been up all night with the baby. What was even more challenging was making [Elle] somebody the audience would like. You look at her, and she's a rich sorority girl who has it all, and you wonder, Who's going to identify with her? So, we worked on making her giving and friendly and likable."[86]

Reese on Body Image

Reese Witherspoon is not a big believer in diets and negative self-image. Instead, the petite actress likes to eat whatever food she is craving and then exercise to counteract the calories. Even so, she has had bouts of self-consciousness during her life. In 1999 she explained this to interviewer Lesley O'Toole of *Express*, and also talked about how she had overcome her feelings of self-doubt:

> The first time I saw myself on screen in *The Man in the Moon*, I was wearing a bathing suit and it was really hard. But it would be really easy to watch yourself in every film and say, "Oh, I look terrible." I think every young actress comes to a point in their life where you decide whether to subscribe to some sort of social standard of what you're supposed to look like. Aesthetics and artificiality make up such a huge part of the industry, so you can either go for that or choose to look the way you do. And I hit that place two or three years ago and opted for the latter.

Witherspoon appears with costar Luke Wilson in a scene from Legally
Blonde. *Though the schedule of shooting the movie was demanding, Reese
enjoyed playing the upbeat Elle Woods.*

Witherspoon also had trouble identifying with the ever positive Elle because the two were not much alike. She says, "I don't
have the kind of self-image that I'm the type of girl that everyone
wants to be friends with. I've always been the kind of person—
even when I was a little girl—who was very independent, always
in my room playing by myself. I see myself as very private and
very quiet. So, Elle was definitely a stretch."[87]

Witherspoon worked on the task of developing her character with first-time feature film director Robert Luketic. The two
got along for the most part, but did have creative differences one
day while working on a scene. Luketic thought Witherspoon had
played the scene perfectly, but she wanted another take because
she thought she could do better. He wanted to move on, and
Witherspoon insisted she get another try. He remembers, "She
got quite upset with me and said, 'How dare you not respect my
decision!' I totally love her, but she will push it as far as the director allows."[88]

Witherspoon did not apologize for her actions. She felt she
had been hired for her opinion of her performance as much as
for the performance itself. "Filmmaking is a collaborative process,"

she explains. "I have things to add, and whether someone chooses to use them is their prerogative. But I'm not going to shut up. . . . I have earned the right to have an opinion, so when people don't listen to me, I get a little pissed off."[89]

Other than that disagreement, making *Legally Blonde* was a great experience for the actress. Elle's positive attitude wore off on her and Witherspoon had fun playing the character. When filming was complete, though, Witherspoon was not sure if her fans would like her in the role or if *Legally Blonde* would do well at the box office. And nothing prepared her for the response to the movie once it opened.

Summer of Stardom

Legally Blonde opened in the summer of 2001, but Witherspoon felt the pressure of having the responsibility of a big movie on her shoulders months before it was released. She told reporters who were wondering how she was handling her first big starring role in a movie, "It's a huge responsibility. It's a big pressure to have it all on you, that's for sure. But I've had a lot of experience leading up to this. Nothing prepares you for it, but you just try to take it in stride."[90]

MGM launched an aggressive media campaign to promote the film. Billboards advertising the movie, showing a coifed, pink-clad Witherspoon, popped up on highways across the country. Witherspoon's friends called and joked that they were sick of looking at her face. Witherspoon, however, was surprised that they even recognized her underneath all the hair and makeup.

She was even more surprised when the movie started making money at the box office, something her films had not done before. *Legally Blonde* grossed more than $100 million worldwide. And reviews of the film, as well as for Witherspoon's performance as Elle, were glowing. Roger Ebert of the *Chicago Sun-Times* raved, "[Witherspoon] is so much the star of the movie that the other actors seem less like co-stars than like partners in an acting workshop, feeding her lines. They percolate, she bubbles. . . . Witherspoon effortlessly animated this material with sunshine and quick wit."[91]

Suddenly, Witherspoon became a Hollywood star. Producers and directors wanted her to be in their movies. Her face was on magazine covers. Reporters clamored for interviews. Fans wanted autographs and pictures of her. It was overwhelming for the actress who had been used to walking down the street unnoticed most days. Witherspoon says:

> This movie definitely struck a chord with people. I was on the set with Ryan while he was [filming in England], and I was always surprised that really refined English actors would come up to me and gush, "I loved *Legally Blonde*." I would say, "You're making fun of me, aren't you?" And they'd say, "No, it's great!" I think the movie expresses a modern feminist attitude. Women aren't just frivolous or studious. They can be girly and accomplished.[92]

Thanks to the film's success, Witherspoon now had her pick of movie scripts. She also had a new asking price per film. She

Witherspoon accepts the Best Comedic Performance award at the 2002 MTV Movie Awards for her role in Legally Blonde.

made $1 million for *Blonde* and rumor had it that she was getting much more for future projects. Some sources reported that she was being offered as much as $15 million per movie.

But just because her paycheck had swelled, Witherspoon was trying to make sure her head did not. She did not spend a lot of time with Hollywood celebrities or go to lots of parties. Instead, she liked to stay close to home and had the same friends she did before she became a superstar. One of the perks of becoming a star, however, was too good for Witherspoon to pass up. She now had her pick of many movie scripts and one, *Sweet Home Alabama*, was especially close to her heart.

Witherspoon's Personal Movie

When Witherspoon was promoting *Legally Blonde*, reporters asked if she had experienced any prejudice as a blonde. Witherspoon replied: "Blonde prejudice, no. But I have had to deal with stereotypes of being southern. People hear a southern accent and automatically figure you have seven children and are barefoot, living on a farm, married to your cousin."[93]

Witherspoon's next film let her break down these stereotypes and led her back to her roots as a southern girl. In *Sweet Home*

Costars Candice Bergen and Patrick Dempsey appear alongside Witherspoon in a scene from the movie Sweet Home Alabama. *Reese's southern roots helped her relate to the character she portrayed.*

Alabama, Witherspoon plays up-and-coming fashion designer Melanie Carmichael. Originally from Alabama, Melanie wants to forget her southern past and the redneck husband she has not seen in seven years. She just wants to live her new life as a New York fashion maven and fiancée of the wealthy son of a political family. But she needs to get divorced from her southern husband before she can remarry, so Melanie has to go home again to convince him to sign the divorce papers.

Unlike Elle and other parts she played, Witherspoon really related to Melanie Carmichael. She remembered moving to California and being embarrassed to tell people where she was from. She also knew what it was like to move far from home, become successful, and then go back home to visit. She says:

> This is the first character I've played that I felt is really close to my own life story and my own personality. She's a Southern girl who moves away and makes an entirely new life for herself in this urban world, then has to go home again. Eventually, she grows to love what's beautiful about the place she came from and recognizes it as part of herself, maybe the best part of herself. That's because it's who she truly is, not what people expect her to be.[94]

Despite knowing just how her character felt, Witherspoon almost did not get the role in *Sweet Home Alabama*. The filmmakers began casting the movie before *Legally Blonde* was released and the producers were worried that Witherspoon was not a big enough star to carry the movie. Screenwriter C. Jay Cox said, "We had talked about Witherspoon early in the project. But there's a limited list of actresses that Hollywood will make romantic comedies with. We said, 'It's too bad Witherspoon isn't on that list.' Then all of a sudden, last summer [2001]—bam!— she was a movie star."[95]

Witherspoon was as excited to play the role as the screenwriters, director, and producers were to see her in it. She had worked with the director, Andy Tennant, ten years before on the television movie *Desperate Choices: To Save My Child*. She liked and respected him a great deal. Witherspoon knew Tennant understood female characters. She also knew that he would be open to her suggestions about how to represent southern people so that they did not come across as ignorant, as she felt they often did in other films. "I wanted to celebrate the eccentricities of southern people because there is a lot of humor there, but also represent the values and morals they have," she says.[96] Tennant accepted many of Witherspoon's suggestions, and the filming of *Sweet Home Alabama* began in the fall of 2001.

"I Just Love Pretending to Vomit!"

Witherspoon enjoyed playing Melanie Carmichael. The character was flawed. She is embarrassed by her family and does not always keep her friends' confidences. In one scene in the film, Melanie reveals a friend's secret she swore to keep. She also throws up after drinking too much. The latter was one of Witherspoon's favorite scenes in the film. She says, "Puking was my favorite thing in the movie! It was corn chowder . . . and we did lots of takes because I was having so much fun. I just love pretending to vomit!"[97]

The cast and crew shot parts of the movie in Georgia and Tennessee, and Witherspoon liked being home and spending time with her family. Her brother John was her chauffeur on the set when they were filming. And Witherspoon claims she got her southern accent back by arguing with him during car rides to and from the set. Of that accent, she says, "When I started acting I was told to lose my accent, or I wouldn't work that much. But I still have it. It comes out whenever I go back home."[98]

Other parts of *Sweet Home Alabama* were filmed in New York City. In fact, the cast was in Manhattan on September 10, 2001,

Witherspoon's Role Models

In the following excerpt from a *USA Today* article, Reese Witherspoon tells journalist Claudia Puig whom she admires in Hollywood:

I was never a 6-5 supermodel babe; I'm a 5-2 little thing. I identify more with the Holly Hunters and the Sally Fields than, say, Michelle Pfeiffer. Those people always represented a real dedication to their work, an incredible work ethic and a lack of vanity. Not that those women aren't beautiful, but it's not what their self-worth is based on. I don't know them personally, but that's the impression I get watching their work. Those were the women I was trying to be like.

filming a scene at the Marc Jacobs fashion show. The next day, on September 11, 2001, America was attacked. Commercial airplanes were hijacked and flown into the World Trade Center's Twin Towers, the Pentagon in Washington, D.C., and a field in Pennsylvania. In total, more than three thousand people died. Like the rest of the world, Witherspoon and the crew were scared about being in New York and worried about what was going to happen next. Despite their fears, the cast and crew decided to continue filming in the city. They were the first. Other production companies soon resumed their plans to film in the city as well.

Witherspoon was also the first actor to host *Saturday Night Live* (which is filmed in New York City) after the attacks. Although she may have been nervous to be there only weeks later, no one would have guessed it from Witherspoon's performances in the comedy sketches. It felt good to laugh with all that was going on in the world, and Witherspoon enjoyed bonding with the cast members.

Breaking Box Office Records

Sweet Home Alabama broke box office records when it was released in September 2002. It earned more than $35 million in its opening weekend, making it the biggest September opening of a movie in history as well as the best-ever romantic comedy debut.

Reviews for the film were mixed, but Witherspoon received her fair share of praise. *US Weekly* film critic Thelma Adams said: "Witherspoon is an American sweetheart with a modern edge."[99] And *Entertainment Weekly* called her "a genuinely attractive performer . . . [p]inning her easy, roll-with-the-punches performance between gestures of city elegance and those of country spunk."[100]

But even more important to Witherspoon were her costars' words of admiration. Josh Lucas, who plays Melanie's southern husband, was impressed with Witherspoon. He says, "The thing about Reese is that she's massively intelligent and she knows her job like the back of her hand. She comes in with a level of preparation which is awesome. She's as comedically sharp as they get."[101]

Patrick Dempsey, who plays Andrew, Melanie's northern fiancé, says Witherspoon was wise beyond her years. But what he found most amazing about her was a quality he could not quite define. "I don't know what it is, but there is something magical

The cast of Sweet Home Alabama *(pictured) was in New York City when the devastating terrorist attacks on the World Trade Center occurred on September 11, 2001.*

about her. The camera loves her. She has a lot of depth and strength of character and I think that translates into the characters that she plays. They're strong and edgy, interesting women. I think that's part of the appeal. I think that women love that about her, and men find that really attractive. She has that indefinable something—that movie star quality."[102]

Hollywood Star

Audiences agreed with Dempsey that Witherspoon had movie-star quality. With two hits in a row, Witherspoon was now a star. And suddenly, many people wanted to get to know her. But Witherspoon was wary about whom she formed close relationships with. She often wondered if people genuinely liked her or if they were drawn to the star she had become. She claimed she was lucky to have friends who knew her before *Legally Blonde*. She reveals, "I certainly think there's a point in your career when you start to feel like the gates of your friendship are closing. And whoever's on the inside is going to be there for life; whoever's on the outside, it's going to be a little bit harder to get in. I try to be as open as I can, but you have to be very discerning and be a pretty good judge of character to see what people want from you."[103]

What many people wanted was for Witherspoon to attend their parties or premieres. She was being invited to more Hollywood premieres and parties than ever before. While she preferred to keep a low profile most of the time, Witherspoon and Phillippe did dress up for each other's premieres and went to some of the big awards shows. For example, they attended the 2002 Academy Awards, where together they presented an award for best makeup.

Rumors of competition between the couple surfaced after Phillippe joked during the awards ceremony that Witherspoon should open the envelope and read the winner since she made more money than he did. It was an offhand comment that neither of them took seriously even though the press hinted at his feeling resentful. Witherspoon explains, "It shows how comfortable he is with it. Anyway, the next day it'll be him making more money than me. You're up, you're down, but no matter what, we're together."[104]

Phillippe agreed and in an interview with Jeremy Helligar of *US Weekly* he clarifies what he meant by his onstage joke. "I am so happy for my wife," he says. "I am ecstatic that she makes more than most men in Hollywood. . . . I am not competitive. She is more competitive than [I am]. She needs my help and support.

In Therapy

Although they are happily married, Ryan Phillippe and Reese Witherspoon admit that they have problems just like any other couple. And in August 2002 Phillippe revealed to a reporter that he and Witherspoon individually see therapists in an effort to make their marriage stronger. Phillippe told Ann Oldenburg of *USA Today*:

It's tough to be young and it's tough to be married. We each individually go to therapy. Why make people feel as if working on themselves or working on their relationship is a negative thing? The biggest mistake is not doing that, ignoring it, and having the marriage fall apart because of laziness. [Counseling has helped me because] of how internalized I tend to be and how moody I am. At times in my life, I have been prone to depression. That's why I have made therapy part of my life. And I think it enhances my relationships with my wife and daughter as well.

We are more connected now because you rely on that person to be your rock when everyone is so fake or after you for your earning potential."[105]

In fact, Witherspoon's earning potential had skyrocketed in just a couple of years, and critics wondered where she was headed in terms of material. Hollywood producers and directors as well as critics were questioning the choices she was making. No one doubted her talent but many noticed that she was no longer making as many independent films as she once had.

Robert Thompson, a professor of media and pop culture at Syracuse University, had his own theory about the choices Witherspoon was making and how they would affect her career in the years to come. Thompson told the *Toronto Star,* "As she creates her career, she'll realize that a great actor's career is made on a couple of things: Number one, being in a few great movies, and number two, being in a few huge movies. I'm sure she's looking at that right now. . . . The next three years, and three films, are crucial to her career. Whatever those next three movies are will establish a pattern, and that becomes the stuff that reputations are made of."[106]

Chapter 6

The Importance of Being Reese

THE NEXT ROLE Reese Witherspoon had decided to take was a complete departure from both Elle Woods and Melanie Carmichael. She decided to play Cecily Cardew in a film adaptation of the play *The Importance of Being Earnest* written by Oscar Wilde.

This film and others continue to keep her busy, but Witherspoon has managed to find a good balance between work and home. And in addition to making movies and being a wife and mother, Witherspoon is also involved in several charities and has her own production company, Type A Films.

Witherspoon realizes how lucky she is, but she also knows that fame can be fleeting. "It can all go away as fast as it came," she says of her career, "so it's really important to me to find my personal happiness in other places."[107]

Living and Filming in England

Witherspoon was thrilled when her personal and professional worlds collided in 2001. Both she and Ryan Phillippe were asked to make movies in England at the same time. Phillippe was set to film *Gosford Park* with an impressive cast that included Helen Mirren, Maggie Smith, and Jeremy Northam, while Witherspoon had signed on to make *The Importance of Being Earnest* with Colin Firth and Rupert Everett.

Usually, the two take turns making movies so one of them can always be at home with Ava. They also make sure that they are never apart from each other for more than two weeks. But these projects presented them with the opportunity to work and be there for their daughter at the end of the day.

Ryan Phillippe and Helen Mirren appear in a scene from Gosford Park, *a movie shot in England. Ryan and Reese lived in England while working on different films.*

So, for a few months in 2001, the whole family temporarily set up residence in England. Two-year-old Ava adapted to the new country right away. She even picked up the accent and expressions. She called her stroller by the English term, "pushchair."

Witherspoon, however, had a more difficult time. She needed to have a convincing British accent for her role and it was harder to learn than Witherspoon had imagined. "I hadn't done a lot of period stuff, and I saw it as a challenge. It was a good way to initiate myself to a foreign accent but not have the lead in the film. I worked on the accent every day, for six weeks. I worked really hard, because you know you can sink or swim in these situations."[108]

Luckily, Witherspoon did not sink. She worked hard to master the accent, and to understand how to play Cecily. Her castmates and director Oliver Parker were impressed by her efforts. Parker says:

Cecily is one of the trickier parts to cast, because very often it can be an irritating character. It's meant to have a youthfulness and strength, but usually you get someone too old. This is a sweet young thing, but the more you get to know her, the more you realize there's a really tenacious, wise creature in there. There are very few actors Witherspoon's age with that sort of maturity. You've got to have someone who has a sort of blazing intelligence without showing it off. And she is extremely smart, as you know. . . . It's a very daunting prospect, slotting into this thing, which is on the whole a very British possession, and to come in as an outsider, especially where you are surrounded by the likes of Judi Dench. But Reese is a terrific little impressionist. She works like crazy, and she is meticulous—something of a perfectionist. I don't think she would have taken it on unless she thought she could get there.[109]

Costar Frances O'Connor was equally enthusiastic about both Witherspoon's personality and acting abilities. She says, "Reese

Witherspoon with costar Rupert Everett in a scene from The Importance of Being Earnest. *Reese spent weeks mastering a British accent for the film.*

is not pretending to be anything she's not, and I think that's really refreshing. She came up with the goods."[110]

Despite Witherspoon's (and the rest of the cast's) hard work on the film, it did not do well at the box office. The movie was not available in wide release and did not play on very many movie screens. But because it was released just a couple of months before *Sweet Home Alabama* and Witherspoon was not the star, it did not seem to soil her reputation. She remained in a position where she could pick and choose her projects.

Type A Films

In order to work on projects she liked, Witherspoon had started her own production company in 2000. She had a partner, Debra Siegel, and their company was called Type A Films after Witherspoon's childhood nickname, Little Type A. Witherspoon wanted her company to make quality films women, especially young women, would enjoy, something she feels is lacking in many films today. "There's a female attitude that isn't necessarily represented in a lot of movies," Witherspoon explains.[111]

Reese's Type A Personality

Reese Witherspoon has had the drive to succeed from the time she was a little girl. Although her personality has helped gain tremendous success, Witherspoon admits that sometimes it can also be unhealthy. She told reporter Krista Smith of *Vanity Fair* magazine:

My parents used to call me Little Type A. I was always very busy and driven. Part of that is great, and part of that can tear you up. . . . Why at the age of 14, did I decide to become a professional? . . . It seems bizarre to me to think about a 14-year-old doing the things I did. I'm starting to learn that the pace at which I run is not conducive to a healthy life. I've worked hard and pushed myself hard, and . . . in the end something is going to crack. I don't know what it is yet. I am just figuring this out about myself . . . and I am starting to learn to pull back. I'm trying to take those moments where everything is going well and and enjoy them. That's why I thank God that Ryan and I got married. There are times when you think, Are these the right decisions that I'm making? Ultimately, I think it has been really helpful to have the person who knows me so well for a husband, who experiences the same kind of frustrations and lives the same lifestyle.

Initially, Witherspoon partnered with the movie company Intermedia Film. The two signed a contract giving Intermedia the option to produce and financially back any project Witherspoon decides to make. The company also had the option to pass, if they chose. In October 2002, when that contract expired, Witherspoon signed a similar one with Universal Pictures.

Type A Films' first project is the sequel to *Legally Blonde.* The movie is entitled *Legally Blonde 2: Red, White and Blonde,* and is set for a July 2003 release. The new film will follow Elle Woods as she moves to Washington, D.C., and gets involved with politics. Witherspoon says, "I was attracted to the idealistic quality of Elle's character and am happy to get back into her shoes. Kate Kondell's script is great. It puts a positive spin on politics today. I look forward to inspiring young people to be interested in government."[112]

Witherspoon has several other projects in various stages of development. These include a movie about female tennis players, an adaptation of a 1960s television show about a private investigator named Honey West, and a film based on two stories from the popular Melissa Banks book entitled *The Girl's Guide to Hunting and Fishing.* Witherspoon is excited about these new projects and eager to work on them. She explains, "I've never been a producer before, so it's been really fun finding a writer and listening to people's ideas."[113]

Reese's Causes

Witherspoon's desire to be successful extends beyond acting. She is dedicated to various causes and charities. She and Ryan Phillippe hosted a benefit for the Rape Treatment Center in Los Angeles in September 2002. They are also both supporters of educational scholarships. "Education is a big thing for us," Witherspoon explains. "I have a couple of scholarships that I've started on my own with schools back in Tennessee. Ryan and I want to create opportunities for kids who work hard but don't necessarily have the monetary means of financing an education."[114]

But the cause most important to Witherspoon's heart is the issue of gun control reform. She feels it is too easy for children to get their hands on guns and for anyone to buy a gun in the United States. Because of her concern, Witherspoon was a supporter of the Million Mom March. On Mother's Day in 2000, the actress joined mothers from all over the world in a march in Washington, D.C. She and the other marchers were calling for mandatory licensing and registration of all handguns and child-safety trigger locks. Her own mother, Betty, joined her, as did many celebrities including Susan Sarandon, Melissa Etheridge, Courtney Love, Rosie O'Donnell, and Hillary Rodham Clinton. Witherspoon was awed by the crowd and proud of the cause they were supporting. She also claimed to be filled with hope "because when this many women get together, great things will happen."[115]

Witherspoon decided to join the march after watching news stories of shooting deaths involving kids. One child, six-year-old Kayla Rolland, was shot by a classmate. Others were killed at Columbine High School and at a day camp in California. "What's happening in a country where a 6-year-old shoots another 6-year-old?" she asked. "Those of us who are lucky enough to only read about these tragedies in the paper have to get involved. It's time for us to march."[116]

Witherspoon kept a diary of her experiences at the event that was published in *US Weekly* magazine. She hoped that other moth-

Witherspoon and Phillippe pose at a fundraising event to benefit college-bound minority students.

The Million Mom March Diary

Reese Witherspoon kept a journal of her experiences at the May 2000 Million Mom March for *US Weekly* magazine. Here are some excerpts from her article "If You Believe in Something, You Have to Speak Out":

At 9 A.M. we arrive on the Mall [in Washington, D.C.]. The weather has changed overnight—we've been blessed with a beautiful spring day (Mom wasn't worried about the heat—she says we southern girls can take it). We gather with other celebrities for a group portrait. There are so many famous, accomplished women here today that we joke that the air is filled with estrogen! Susan Sarandon, Bette Midler, Rosie O'Donnell, Melissa Etheridge, Courtney Love . . . it's an amazing group. Earlier, I talked with Susan about her last big demonstration in Washington. She came to march for abortion rights in 1988, when she was pregnant with one of her three children. Now she's back with her daughter, Eva. It's wonderful to see her commitment to social change—she's a real role model.

11:30 A.M. After the photo, we join a "stroller march" down the Mall. There are more people here than I've ever seen in my life. I try to take in all the personal messages people have on their banners and the pictures of children who have been lost to gun violence. Hillary Rodham Clinton arrives and the front line of marchers with whom I'm walking just disintegrates around her. Women are shouting "She's my senator! She's my senator!" My mother is screaming "There she is! There she is!" Everyone is trying to get a peek at her. I'm in awe.

3 P.M. We hear that 750,000 people are here today representing the mothers of America—the largest gun-control rally in history. I get the chance to meet [gun-control advocate] James Brady and tell him how great I think today is and that I'm so glad he could be here to speak with us. I talk to Melissa Etheridge and Julie Cypher, two very smart women who really care about the safety of their children and everyone's children, and later I listen to a moving song by Emmylou Harris, which contains the lyrics, "I've got a heart full of fear/and I offer it up on this altar of tears." Before I know it, it's my turn onstage to introduce [Bobby] Brown [a seventeen-year-old who was paralyzed in a drive-by shooting]. I'm nervous speaking in front of thousands of people, but it's exhilarating.

ers would read about her experiences and find out more about gun control and how to protect their children. "I couldn't pass up an opportunity to use my celebrity for a cause I believe in deeply," Witherspoon says.[117]

Although the public considers her a movie star, Reese Witherspoon prefers to define herself as a wife, mother, and activist.

Reese's Rules of Fashion and Beauty

Witherspoon may not care as deeply about fashion as she does about gun control, but she does have a weakness for clothes and shoes. "She likes makeup, she's very into clothes and bags, and she's always breaking open some new lipstick she just bought," says her friend, costume designer Sophie da Rakoff Carbonell.

"She's a Grace Kelly in blue jeans—classic and sophisticated but a totally modern girl."[118]

She claims to have been more of a clotheshorse and shopper before Ava was born, however. Before she had a baby, Witherspoon bought designer labels that were dry-clean only. Her clothes are now more practical—and made of machine-washable fabrics. Her style today is "simple, comfortable. I have to have very washable clothes because I have a three-year-old and at any moment I can be attacked with a peanut butter and jelly sandwich," she says.[119]

When she does shop, Witherspoon prefers stores like Gap, J. Crew, Banana Republic, Club Monaco, and Old Navy. She also likes the Juicy Couture label and designer Marni, whose clothes Witherspoon has called her weakness and has compared to art. However, she is not a label snob. Witherspoon prefers a white T-shirt, jeans, and Converse All-Stars to just about anything else.

She does sometimes dress up, though, usually for a Hollywood party or premiere. On these occasions, Witherspoon usually creates a sensation because she is so well dressed. In fact, she was on many "best-dressed" lists after the 2002 Oscars when she wore a vintage black lace Christian Dior gown.

In addition to having fashion rules, Witherspoon also has a beauty regimen. She wears sunscreen each and every day and

Ms. Manners

Reese Witherspoon has a reputation for being polite. She grew up taking etiquette classes and learning how to write thank-you notes. And she believes a guest should never arrive at a dinner party without a gift for the host. Friends and coworkers revealed their thoughts on Witherspoon's manners to *People* magazine, which profiled Witherspoon as one of the "50 Most Beautiful People" in 2003. Costume designer Sophie da Rakoff Carbonell claims, "She has impeccable manners. You always get a thank-you note, she remembers everyone's birthdays and special occasions." Marc Platt, producer of *Legally Blonde 2,* says, "When we were filming, every two weeks, there was some kind of gift from Reese to the crew. One day she'd have a blended-drink truck making drinks for everyone, then a mariachi band or karaoke, just as her way of saying thank you." And Bob Newhart, Witherspoon's costar on *Legally Blonde 2* remembers, "The crew just loved her. She knew the name of everybody on the set and what was going on in their lives, and that's important to people."

wishes she had started protecting her skin earlier. She also drinks lots of water and does not smoke. She enjoys getting massages, manicures, and pedicures and having her hair cut.

The Future

Witherspoon has many plans for the future but they do not all revolve around movies. She says, "I really have a lot of other interests. I wanted to go to medical school for a while and I still have a hankering to study psychiatry. I think you really need to find your passion in life and I'm not convinced that acting is mine."[120]

Right now, though, acting remains her primary career, and Witherspoon has been busy. In May 2003, after filming the sequel to *Legally Blonde*, Witherspoon relocated to England again to start filming the period piece *Vanity Fair*. Director Mira Nair chose Witherspoon for the role of Becky Sharp because of the actress's tremendous appeal. Nair says, "The ability, like Becky, to be the same with the courtiers as she is with the king [is like] the democracy of Reese. She appeals to the kid in the shopping mall as well as to royalty."[121]

In addition to *Vanity Fair*, Witherspoon has chosen to work on two other films—*Whiteout* in which she will play a U.S. marshal tracking a killer in Antarctica and *Walk the Line*, a movie about country singer Johnny Cash. In the latter, Witherspoon will star as Cash's wife, singer-songwriter June Carter.

Witherspoon would also like to team up with her husband onscreen again. She enjoyed making *Cruel Intentions* with him and admires his acting abilities. She explains, "I would love to work with him again. I would love for us to have a . . . relationship where

Ryan on Reese

Ryan Phillippe admits that maintaining a marriage in Hollywood can be difficult, but he and Reese Witherspoon are determined to succeed. He told reporter Krista Smith of *Vanity Fair* magazine in June 2002, "She constantly keeps me excited and engaged, and I'm always interested to hear what's on her mind. We try to be as mutually supportive as possible, but it is incredibly taxing because of our schedules and all the obstacles inherent in living out a relationship in the public eye. Our lives are complicated, but we make the effort."

we could work together as different characters and in different contexts."[122]

But the couple decided to have another baby before they made another movie together. Witherspoon is expecting her second child in the fall of 2003. She looks forward to expanding her family.

In addition to acting and being a parent, Witherspoon wants to direct someday. Her perfectionistic qualities and eye for detail make her an excellent candidate for that job. Alexander Payne, Witherspoon's director in *Election*, says, "[S]he can do anything. But it kind of scares me that she wants to direct, because she'll push all the rest of us off."[123]

Whether directing, acting, parenting, or doing something else entirely, Witherspoon remains driven and ambitious. She is willing to work hard to achieve her goals. "Nobody made Julia Roberts a star. She busted her butt," Witherspoon says. "She broke down stereotypes and believed in herself. That's the kind of tenacity I think it takes to succeed."[124] And success is something that Reese Witherspoon knows well.

Notes

Introduction: America's Newest Sweetheart

1. Quoted in Jeremy Helligar, "Woman on Top," *US Weekly*, October 7, 2002, p. 54.
2. Quoted in Jill Smolowe, "The Essential Reese," *People*, October 4, 2002. www.people.aol.com.
3. Quoted in Helligar, "Woman on Top," p. 54.

Chapter 1: Sweet Home Tennessee

4. Quoted in Claudia Puig, "Witherspoon's 'Sweet Home,'" *USA Today*, Life Section, September 19, 2002, p. 1.
5. Quoted in Helligar, "Woman on Top," p. 54.
6. Quoted in Puig, "Witherspoon's 'Sweet Home,'" p. 1.
7. Quoted in Chris Schlegel, "Q&A with Reese Witherspoon," E!Online, July 10, 2001. www.eonline.com.
8. Quoted in Krista Smith, "Belle du Jour," *Vanity Fair*, June 2002, p. 174.
9. Quoted in J.V. McAuley, "Home Life with Reese Witherspoon: Mom, Actress, 'Honey West,'" *Zap2It*, July 13, 2001.
10. Quoted in Helligar, "Woman on Top," p. 54.
11. Quoted in Sheryl Berk, "Reese Witherspoon," *Biography*, June 2002, p. 40.
12. Quoted in Barry Koltnow, "Reese Witherspoon Gets Ready to Juggle Family Concerns, Busy Film Schedule," *Orange County Register*, May 3, 1999.
13. The Reese Witherspoon Collection, "Biography." www.geocities.com.

14. Quoted in Koltnow, "Reese Witherspoon Gets Ready to Juggle Family Concerns, Busy Film Schedule."
15. Quoted in Berk, "Reese Witherspoon," p. 38.
16. Quoted in Helligar, "Woman on Top," p. 51.
17. Quoted in Helligar, "Woman on Top," p. 51.
18. Quoted in Helligar, "Woman on Top," p. 51.

Chapter 2: Actress and Student

19. Quoted in Jennifer Kasle Furmaniak, "The Reason Reese Is Reveling," *Cosmopolitan,* July 2001, p. 171.
20. Quoted in Furmaniak, "The Reason Reese Is Reveling," p. 171.
21. The Reese Witherspoon Collection, "Biography."
22. James Berardinelli, "*Freeway*, A Film Review," ReelViews. http://movie-reviews.colossus.net.
23. Quoted in Kate Meyers, "The Gauge of Innocence," *Entertainment Weekly*, October 11, 1996, p. 99.
24. Quoted in Meyers, "The Gauge of Innocence," p. 99.
25. Quoted in Josh Rottenberg, "As Good As It Gets," *InStyle*, October 2002, p. 460.
26. Quoted in J.V. McAuley, "Reese Witherspoon: The Myth of the Dumb Blonde Smashed!" *Zap2It,* July 13, 2001.
27. Quoted in Meyers, "The Gauge of Innocence," p. 99.
28. Quoted in McAuley, "Reese Witherspoon: The Myth of the Dumb Blonde Smashed!"
29. Quoted in McAuley, "Reese Witherspoon: The Myth of the Dumb Blonde Smashed!"
30. Quoted in Berk, "Reese Witherspoon," p. 39.
31. Quoted in Sean M. Smith, "Reese Witherspoon Lets Down Her Hair," *Premiere*, August 2001, p. 102.
32. Quoted in Sean Macauley, "The Bionic Blonde Next Door," *Times* (London), October 25, 2001, p. 14.
33. Quoted in Krista Smith, "Belle du Jour," p. 178.
34. Quoted in E!Online, "The Sizzlin Sixteen '99." www.eonline.com.

Chapter 3: Coming into Her Own

35. Quoted in Berk, "Reese Witherspoon," p. 39.
36. Quoted in Krista Smith, "Belle du Jour," p. 233.

37. Quoted in Rottenberg, "As Good As It Gets," p. 460.

38. Quoted in Macauley, "The Bionic Blonde Next Door," p. 14.

39. Quoted in Rottenberg, "As Good As It Gets," p. 460.

40. Quoted in Furmaniak, "The Reason Reese Is Reveling," p. 172.

41. Quoted in Elizabeth Kuster, "Reese's Pieces," *CosmoGirl!* August 2001. www.geocities.com.

42. Quoted in David Lipsky, "Hollywood's Golden Couple," *TV Guide Ultimate Cable*, September 18–24, 1999. www.geocities.com.

43. Quoted in Krista Smith, "Belle du Jour," p. 233.

44. Quoted in Berk, "Reese Witherspoon," p. 40.

45. Quoted in Lipsky, "Hollywood's Golden Couple."

46. Quoted in Lipsky, "Hollywood's Golden Couple."

47. Quoted in *Entertainment Tonight*, "ET Spotlight Interview with Tobey Maguire and Reese Witherspoon," October 15, 1998. www.geocities.com.

48. Quoted in Rottenberg, "As Good As It Gets," p. 460.

49. Quoted in Smith, "Reese Witherspoon Lets Down Her Hair," p. 49.

50. Quoted in Charles Taylor, "Exile in *Pleasantville*," *Salon*, October 23, 1998. www.salon.com.

51. Quoted in Koltnow, "Reese Witherspoon Gets Ready to Juggle Family Concerns, Busy Film Schedule."

52. Quoted in Smith, "Reese Witherspoon Lets Down Her Hair," p. 49.

53. Quoted in Smith, "Reese Witherspoon Lets Down Her Hair," p. 49.

54. Quoted in Stephen Schaefer, "*Cruel Intentions'* Straitlaced Schoolgirl Rocks the Vote in *Election*," Mr. Showbiz, April 21, 1999. www.geocities.com.

55. Quoted in Stephan Tally, "Reese at Peace," *Time Out New York*, April 15–22, 1999. www.geocities.com.

56. Quoted in *Election* Production Notes. www.geocities.com.

57. Quoted in Smith, "Reese Witherspoon Lets Down Her Hair," p. 49.

58. Quoted in Roger Ebert, "*Election*," *Chicago Sun-Times*, April 4, 1999. www.suntimes.com.

59. Quoted in E!Online, "The Sizzlin Sixteen '99."

60. Quoted in Schaefer, "*Cruel Intentions'* Straitlaced Schoolgirl Rocks the Vote in *Election*."

61. Quote in Liane Bonin, "Blonde Ambition," *Flaunt*, August 2001. www.geocities.com.

62. Quoted in Bonin, "Blonde Ambition."

Chapter 4: Putting Family First

63. Quoted in Brian D. Johnson, "Cool Intentions," *Maclean's*, March 22, 1999, p. 50.

64. Quoted in Rebecca Mead, "Great Expectations," *Allure*, May 1999. www.geocities.com.

65. Quoted in Mead, "Great Expectations."

66. Quoted in James Berardinelli, "*Best Laid Plans*, A Film Review," ReelViews," http.//movie-reviews.colossus.net.

67. Quoted in Jim Slotek, "Reese Argues for *American Psycho*," *Toronto Sun*, February 24, 1999. www.geocities.com.

68. Quoted in Lesley O'Toole, "Reese Witherspoon Interview," *Express*, September 18, 1999. www.geocities.com.

69. Quoted in Bob Strauss, "Reese's Thesis," *Daily News Los Angeles*, May 10, 1999. www.geocities.com.

70. Quoted in Rottenberg, "As Good As It Gets," p. 467.

71. Reese Witherspoon, "That Glow: Reese Witherspoon Tells It Like It Is," 1999. www.geocities.com.

72. Quoted in Rottenberg, "As Good As It Gets," p. 467.

73. Quoted in Furmaniak, "The Reason Reese Is Reveling," p. 172.

74. Quoted in Furmaniak, "The Reason Reese Is Reveling," p. 172.

75. Reese Witherspoon, interview by Jay Leno, *The Tonight Show with Jay Leno*, February 1, 2000. www.geocities.com.

76. Quoted in AOL Chat, July 19, 2001. www.geocities.com.

77. Quoted in Berk, "Reese Witherspoon," p. 41.

78. Quoted in Merle Ginsberg, "Nouveau Reese," September 2002, p. 420.

79. Quoted in Rottenberg, "As Good as It Gets," p. 467.

80. Quoted in McAuley, "Home Life with Reese Witherspoon."

81. Quoted in Rottenberg, "As Good as It Gets," p. 467.

82. Quoted in Smolowe, "The Essential Reese."

Chapter 5: Commercial Success

83. Quoted in Jeff Dawson, "Princess Screwball," *Times* (London), December 14, 2002, p. 42.

84. Quoted in *Teenmag.com*, "Reese Is the Word." www.geocities.com.

85. Quoted in Schlegel, "Q&A with Reese Witherspoon," p. 1.

86. Quoted in Smith, "Reese Witherspoon Lets Down Her Hair," p. 102.

87. Quoted in Smith, "Reese Witherspoon Lets Down Her Hair," p. 102.

88. Quoted in Smith, "Reese Witherspoon Lets Down Her Hair," p. 102.

89. Quoted in Schlegel, "Q&A with Reese Witherspoon," p. 2.

90. Quoted in Schlegel, "Q&A with Reese Witherspoon," p. 3.

91. Roger Ebert, "*Legally Blonde*," *Chicago Sun-Times*, July 13, 2001. www.suntimes.com.

92. Quoted in Berk, "Reese Witherspoon," p. 42.

93. Quoted in Schlegel, "Q&A with Reese Witherspoon," p. 1.

94. Quoted in Berk, "Reese Witherspoon," p. 42.

95. Quoted in Nancy Miller, "Blonde Bombshell," *Entertainment Weekly*. www.ew.com.

96. Quoted in Christina Radish, "Reese the Romantic," FilmStew.com. www.geocities.com.

97. Quoted in Ginsberg, "Nouveau Reese," p. 420.

98. Quoted in Schlegel, "Q&A with Reese Witherspoon," p. 1.

99. Thelma Adams, "Home, Sweet Home," *US Weekly*, October 7, 2002, p. 72.

100. Lisa Schwartzbaum, "Belle Weathered," *Entertainment Weekly*, October 4, 2002, p. 124.

101. Quoted in Radish, "Reese the Romantic."

102. Quoted in Radish, "Reese the Romantic."

103. Quoted in Nina Burleigh, "Natural Blonde," *US Weekly*, July 30, 2001. www.geocities.com.

104. Quoted in Rottenberg, "As Good As It Gets," p. 467.

105. Quoted in Helligar, "Woman on Top," p. 52.

106. Quoted in Murray Whyte, "Will the Real Reese Please Stand Up?" *Toronto Star*, October 1, 2002, p. D05.

Chapter 6: The Importance of Being Reese

107. Quoted in O'Toole, "Reese Witherspoon Interview."

108. Quoted in Smith, "Belle du Jour," p. 177.

109. Quoted in Smith, "Belle du Jour," p. 177.

110. Quoted in Smith, "Belle du Jour," p. 177.

111. Quoted in Rebecca Ascher-Walsh, "Reel World," *Entertainment Weekly*, November 9, 2001, p. 80.

112. Quoted in Joal Ryan, "Reese: It Pays to Be Blonde," E!Online, September 5, 2002. www.eonline.com.

113. Quoted in Liane Bonin, "Blonde on Blonde." *Entertainment Weekly*. www.ew.com.

114. Quoted in Smith, "Belle du Jour," p. 234.

115. Quoted in J.D. Heyman, "Million Mom March: The Inside Story," *US Weekly*, May 29, 2000. www.geocities.com.

116. Reese Witherspoon, "If You Believe in Something You Have to Speak Out," *US Weekly*, May 29, 2000. www.geocities.com.

117. Witherspoon, "If You Believe in Something You Have to Speak Out."

118. Quoted in *People*, "50 Most Beautiful People," May 12, 2003.

119. Quoted in Geri Richter Campbell, "17 Minutes with Reese," *Seventeen*, October 2002. www.geocities.com.

120. Quoted in O'Toole, "Reese Witherspoon Interview."

121. Quoted in Miller, "Blonde Bombshell."

122. Quoted in Mead, "Great Expectations."

123. Quoted in Smith, "Belle du Jour," p. 234.

124. Quoted in Smolowe, "The Essential Reese."

Important Dates in the Life of Reese Witherspoon

1976
Laura Jean Reese Witherspoon is born in New Orleans, Louisiana, on March 22.

1981
The Witherspoon family moves to Nashville, Tennessee.

1983
Reese appears in a local television commercial and decides she would like to be an actress.

1990
Reese gets the lead in the film *The Man in the Moon* and spends her summer break making the movie.

1994
Reese graduates from the Harpeth Hall School in Nashville and is accepted at Stanford University. She delays enrolling for a year to make the films *Freeway* and *Fear*.

1995–1996
Reese attends Stanford University and makes the film *Overnight Delivery* during winter break. Leaves Stanford in the fall of 1996 to move to Los Angeles.

1997
Meets Ryan Phillippe at twenty-first birthday party. They move in together later that year. Wins Best Actress prize at the Catalonian (Spain) International Film Festival for *Freeway*.

1998

Films *Twilight* and *Pleasantville* are released. Wins Movieline Young Hollywood Award for Best Female Breakthrough Performance for *Twilight*.

1999

Cruel Intentions, Election, Best Laid Plans, and *American Psycho* are released. Reese is nominated for a Golden Globe Award and wins the National Society of Film Critics Award and the Online Film Critics Society Award for Best Actress for *Election*. Marries Ryan Phillippe on June 5 and daughter Ava is born on September 9.

2000

Forms production company, Type A Productions. Joins in the Million Mom March gun-control rally in Washington, D.C.

2001

Stars in *Legally Blonde*.

2002

Stars in *The Importance of Being Earnest* and *Sweet Home Alabama*.

2003

Stars in *Legally Blonde 2: Red, White and Blonde* and *Vanity Fair*.

For Further Reading

Books

Ursula Rivera, *Reese Witherspoon*. New York: Childrens Press, 2003. This book, for readers ages nine to twelve, chronicles the life of the actress.

L. Gordon Tait, *The Piety of John Witherspoon: Pew, Pulpit, and Public Forum.* Louisville, KY: Geneva, 2000. This biography of John Witherspoon covers his life and times.

Websites

Glamour Reese Witherspoon (www.reese-witherspoon.org). A site for Reese Witherspoon fans that features news about the actress.

The Reese Witherspoon Collection (www.geocities.com). A comprehensive site covering Reese's life and work, including production notes from her films as well as articles, interviews, and a biography.

Works Consulted

Periodicals

Thelma Adams, "Home, Sweet Home," *US Weekly*, October 7, 2002.

Rebecca Ascher-Walsh, "Reel World," *Entertainment Weekly*, November 9, 2001.

Joey Bartolomeo, "Reese and Ryan: They're Having a Baby!" *US Weekly*, April 14, 2003.

Sheryl Berk, "Reese Witherspoon," *Biography*, June 2002.

Sean Daly, "Phillippe Learns to Swim with Sharks," *Toronto Star*, September 5, 2002.

Jeff Dawson, "Princess Screwball," *Times* (London), December 14, 2002.

Jennifer Kasle Furmaniak, "The Reason Reese Is Reveling," *Cosmopolitan*, July 2001.

Jeff Giles and Devin Gordon, "Reese on Earth," *Newsweek*, April 26, 1999.

Merle Ginsberg, "Nouveau Reese," *W*, September 2002.

Jeremy Helligar, "Woman on Top," *US Weekly*, October 7, 2002.

Brian D. Johnson, "Cool Intentions," *Maclean's*, March 22, 1999.

Barry Koltnow, "Reese Witherspoon Gets Ready to Juggle Family Concerns, Busy Film Schedule," *Orange County Register*, May 3, 1999.

Sean Macauley, "The Bionic Blonde Next Door," *Times* (London), October 25, 2001.

J.V. McAuley, "Home Life with Reese Witherspoon: Mom, Actress, 'Honey West,'" *Zap2It*, July 13, 2001.

——, "Reese Witherspoon: The Myth of the Dumb Blonde Smashed!" *Zap2It*, July 13, 2001.

Kate Meyers, "The Gauge of Innocence," *Entertainment Weekly*, October 11, 1996.

People, "50 Most Beautiful People," May 12, 2003.

Claudia Puig, "Witherspoon's 'Sweet Home,'" *USA Today*, September 19, 2002.

Josh Rottenberg, "As Good As It Gets," *InStyle*, October 2002.

Lisa Schwartzbaum, "Belle Weathered," *Entertainment Weekly*, October 4, 2002.

Krista Smith, "Belle du Jour," *Vanity Fair*, June 2002.

Sean M. Smith, "Reese Witherspoon Lets Down Her Hair," *Premiere*, August 2001.

Murray Whyte, "Will the Real Reese Please Stand Up?" *Toronto Star*, October 1, 2002.

Internet Sources

AOL Chat, July 19, 2001. www.geocities.com.

James Berardinelli, "Best Laid Plans, A Film Review," ReelViews. http://movie-reviews.colossus.net.

——, "*Freeway*, A Film Review," ReelViews.http://movie-reviews.colossus.net.

Liane Bonin, "Blonde Ambition," *Flaunt*, August 2001. www.geocities.com.

——, "Blonde on Blonde," *Entertainment Weekly*. www.ew.com.

Nina Burleigh, "Natural Blonde," *US Weekly*, July 30, 2001. www.geocities.com.

Geri Richter Campbell, "17 Minutes with Reese," *Seventeen*, October 2002. www.geocities.com.

Roger Ebert, "*Election*," *Chicago Sun-Times*, April 4, 1999. www.sun times.com.

——, "*Legally Blonde*," *Chicago Sun-Times*, July 13, 2001. www.sun times.com.

Election Production Notes. www.geocities.com.

Entertainment Tonight, "ET Spotlight Interview with Tobey Maguire and Reese Witherspoon," October 15, 1998. www.geocities.com.

E!Online, "The Sizzlin Sixteen '99." www.eonline.com.

J.D. Heyman, "Million Mom March: The Inside Story," *US Weekly*, May 29, 2000. www.geocities.com.

Michelle Keller, "Reese Witherspoon: Rising Star," *Seventeen*, September 1997. www.geocities.com.

Elizabeth Kuster, "Reese's Pieces," *CosmoGirl!* August 2001. www.geo cities.com.

David Lipsky, "Hollywood's Golden Couple," *TV Guide Ultimate Cable*, September 18–24, 1999. www.geocities.com.

Rebecca Mead, "Great Expectations," *Allure*, May 1999. www.geo cities.com.

Nancy Miller, "Blonde Bombshell," *Entertainment Weekly*. www.ew.com.

Lesley O'Toole, "Reese Witherspoon Interview," *Express*, September 18, 1999. www.geocities.com.

Christina Radish, "Reese the Romantic," FilmStew.com. www.geo cities.com.

The Reese Witherspoon Collection, "Biography." www.geocities.com.

Joal Ryan, "Reese: It Pays to Be Blonde," E!Online, September 5, 2002. www.eonline.com.

Stephen Schaefer, "*Cruel Intentions'* Straitlaced Schoolgirl Rocks the Vote in *Election*," Mr. Showbiz, April 21, 1999. www.geocities.com.

Chris Schlegel, "Q&A with Reese Witherspoon," E!Online, July 10, 2001. www.eonline.com.

Jim Slotek, "Reese Argues for *American Psycho*," *Toronto Sun*, February 24, 1999. www.geocities.com.

Jill Smolowe, "The Essential Reese," *People*, October 4, 2002. www. people.aol.com.

Bob Strauss, "Reese's Thesis," *Daily News Los Angeles*, May 10, 1999. www.geocities.com.

Stephan Tally, "Reese at Peace," *Time Out New York*, April 15–22, 1999. www.geocities.com.

Charles Taylor, "Exile in *Pleasantville*," *Salon*, October 23, 1998. www. salon.com.

Teenmag.com, "Reese Is the Word." www.geocities.com.

Reese Witherspoon, "If You Believe in Something You Have to Speak

Out," *US Weekly*, May 29, 2000. www.geocities.com.

——, interview by Jay Leno, *The Tonight Show with Jay Leno*, February 1, 2000. www.geocities.com.

——, interview by Conan O'Brien, *Late Night with Conan O'Brien*, October 10, 1998. www.geocities.com.

——, "That Glow: Reese Witherspoon Tells It Like It Is," 1999. www.geocities.com.

Index

Picture Credits

Cover Image: © Getty Images

© AP Wide World Photos, 61

© Sebastian Artz/Getty Images, 82

© Chicagofilms/Getty Images, 78

© Jeff Christensen/Getty Images, 33

© Classmates.com, 24

© Eric Ford/Online USA/Getty Images, 57

© Getty Images, 52

© Adrees Latif/Reuters/Landov, 84

Library of Congress, 16

© Lawrence Lucier/Getty Images, 13

© Photofest, 19, 22, 27, 28, 31, 34, 39, 42, 44, 47, 48, 54, 60, 65, 67, 70, 74, 79

© Fred Prouser/Reuters/Landov, 69

About the Author

Award-winning author Anne E. Hill has written a dozen biographies and novels for middle-school and teen readers, including three previous titles in Lucent's People in the News series: *Sandra Bullock*, *Drew Barrymore*, and *Sting*. Some of her other nonfiction titles include *Gwyneth Paltrow*, *Cameron Diaz*, and *Denzel Washington*.

A freelance writer for more than six years, Hill graduated magna cum laude with a bachelor's degree in English from Franklin and Marshall College in 1996, where she was a member of the Phi Beta Kappa Society and wrote for *Franklin and Marshall* magazine. She lives outside Philadelphia with her husband George, and son Caleb. A fan of Reese Witherspoon since she saw her in *The Man in the Moon*, Anne's favorite Reese movies (so far) are *The Man in the Moon* and *Legally Blonde*.